Advanced Spanish Prose
Composition

Advanced Spanish Prose Composition

by

CYRIL A. JONES

University Lecturer in Spanish, Fellow of Trinity
College, Oxford

and

ALEC PAYNE

Senior Spanish Master, Oundle School

City of London
Polytechnic Library
School of Business
Studies

OXFORD UNIVERSITY PRESS · 1971

Oxford University Press, Ely House, London W.1

GLASGOW NEW YORK TORONTO MELBOURNE WELLINGTON
CAPE TOWN SALISBURY IBADAN NAIROBI DAR ES SALAAM LUSAKA ADDIS ABABA
BOMBAY CALCUTTA MADRAS KARACHI LAHORE DACCA
KUALA LUMPUR SINGAPORE HONG KONG TOKYO

PRINTED IN GREAT BRITAIN BY
WILLIAM CLOWES AND SONS, LIMITED, LONDON, BECCLES AND COLCHESTER

Preface

To lecturers and teachers seeking new material; to students, whether at the university or at school, equipped to face a challenge, this prose selection is dedicated. For those with fallible memories, there are signposts indicating some of the pitfalls of translation; for the follower of style, there are parallel passages taken from Spanish authors.

The passages are graded according to difficulty, one asterisk indicating first year university level, two, second year and three, third year. But, on the assumption that university entrance candidates are well grounded in grammar, it is felt that all levels are possible with the aid of a dictionary, even before arrival at the university.

Contents

Section II. DESCRIPTIVE

Section III. SOCIAL COMMENT

viii CONTENTS

Section IV. SCIENCE

Section V. PHILOSOPHICAL AND PSYCHOLOGICAL

Section VI. THE ARTS

Section VII. NATURE

Section VIII. PEOPLE

Section IX. HISTORY

APPENDIX

Introduction
by C. A. Jones

It might be an encouragement to those obliged to perform the exercise
of prose composition to know that there are experienced teachers of the
subject who regard it as well-nigh impossible. Why, then, do they
continue to attempt it, and inflict it on others; and what is the use of it?
The answer is that it is still unrivalled as a means not only of learning
and practising the basic principles, rules, and peculiarities of a language,
and of increasing one's knowledge of vocabulary; but it is also a means
of enlarging one's awareness of the linguistic problems which writers
have to face and the ways in which they solve them; and so a means of
enhancing one's appreciation of literature.

Apart from such obvious works of reference as grammars and dictionaries, about which some advice and information are appended to
this introduction, students would be well advised to keep a 'case-book'
containing notes on difficult problems and the solutions which they find
or which are suggested to them. It is largely the contents of such case-
books, kept by myself and by one of my colleagues, Mr. F. W. Hodcroft,
of St. Cross College, Oxford, which form the basis of this introduction,
in which an attempt is made to list not only the things which we ourselves have found difficult, but which over a period of some twenty
years' teaching our pupils have found to be stumbling-blocks. Many but
not all of these difficulties are dealt with in such reference books as
Harmer and Norton's *Manual of Modern Spanish*; but here the in-
tention is to pinpoint the dangers and traps, rather than emphasize the
positive rules. In doing this, one hopes that the impression will not be
created that we are battling against cunning enemies who set out to
prevent the foreigner from having access to the mysteries of their
language. Spaniards are human beings like ourselves, whose language is
a complex instrument which mixes logical principles with apparently
wayward idiosyncrasies just as our own does.

In setting about the task of translation the practice which my colleague
and I have normally followed has been to work with a native speaker
of Spanish; and although the list of names would be too long to quote,
I should like to acknowledge indebtedness to a series of Spanish

University Lecturers at Oxford who have patiently tolerated not only the mangling of their language by both students and teachers, but the searching and sometimes inane questions directed to them about its mysteries. Perhaps when they read what has been noted and remembered of their observations they will be glad that their names have not been included! The procedure that we have adopted is roughly this: the English-speaking teacher and the Spaniard mark the exercises submitted by pupils separately, and both instructors produce a fair copy. The Spaniard also vets the version done by the English teacher for howlers, and the two versions are then read to the class, first the one done by the English, then the one done by the native speaker. (Some examples of what happens are appended to this introduction.) Pupils can then see the difference between the effort of a reasonably well-informed and experienced foreigner and that of a Spaniard. The English teacher explains the difficulties, and discusses them with the Spaniard, who attends the class, commenting generally on common errors, and individually in the case of plain mistakes. It is a long process, but one which one likes to think is interesting as well as worthwhile.

Most of the difficulties encountered over the years have been in dealing with pronouns, adverbs and adverbial phrases, prepositions and prepositional phrases, conjunctions, and of course vocabulary; but there are a few problems connected with the articles, with gender and concord, and with the verb, which perhaps should also be dealt with. We hope it is understood that the points which follow are typical rather than comprehensive.

1. Articles

(a) Sentences rarely begin with unqualified nouns. You will not find, for instance, such a sentence as *Mujeres iban por la calle*. If you cannot put the verb first, use the article or, for example, *algunas*.

(b) The definite article is needed with *todos* before nouns and numerals, e.g. *todos los hombres*, *todos los dos*; but usage sometimes sanctions some exceptions, e.g. *de todos modos*, *de todas [las] maneras*.

(c) An unqualified predicate noun following the verb *ser* generally omits the indefinite article, e.g. *Este hombre es francés*. If the article is used, it indicates that the speaker or writer has a particular example or kind in mind; and this is normally the case when the noun is qualified, e.g. *Este hombre es un francés muy bien conocido*. The indefinite article may be used, as Coester noted in his *Spanish Grammar* (Boston, Ginn & Co., 1912) p. 115, to attribute a given quality to one's character. For example, *Es un cobarde* suggests that he is a regular coward (by nature), while *Es cobarde* indicates that he is a coward in the particular circumstances referred to.

(d) When *como* is used to introduce a noun in apposition to the subject of a sentence, the indefinite article is rarely used, even with a qualified noun, e.g. *Lo hace como profesor calificado en el Derecho.* The insertion of *un* after *como* in these circumstances would imply that he acted like a teacher of law, even though he wasn't one.

(e) The indefinite article is not used before *otro*, and rarely before *cierto*. Incidentally, one might note here that while *tal*='such a', *un tal* means *cierto*.

(f) The definite article is used in preference to the possessive adjective when referring to parts of the body, articles of clothing, etc., e.g. *Se lavó las manos, se puso los guantes.* The use of the possessive adjective in these circumstances seems to a Spaniard redundant, unless it is intended to give special emphasis to the fact that the article is his or hers, rather than someone else's.

2. Gender

(a) Beware of a group of nouns of Greek origin ending in -*a*, which in spite of the usual rules concerning gender, are masculine. The best thing is to learn them. *The Spanish Academy Grammar* lists thirty-one, among which the most common are: *anagrama, apotegma, axioma, clima, diafragma, dilema, diploma, drama, enigma, epigrama, idioma, mapa, melodrama, monograma, panorama, planeta, poema, problema, programa, síntoma, sistema, telegrama* (page 14). One should add at least two: *tema* and *esquema*.

(b) *Mar* and *arte*, although usually masculine, can be feminine, *mar* generally among seafaring people, who perhaps unchivalrously notice the unpredictable quality of the element with which they have so much contact, e.g. *alta mar*; and *arte* usually in the plural, e.g. *las bellas artes*.

(c) Adjectives ending in anything but -*o* are invariable for gender except -*án*, -*ón*, -*ete*, -*ote*, -*ín*, -*or* (the last only when used as a noun, e.g. *la superiora*), and certain adjectives of nationality (e.g. *inglesa*, but *una mujer cortés*. It is interesting to note that while *provenzal* is invariable for gender, *andaluz* is not.

(d) When a feminine or plural noun is preceded by *más* the adjective *mucho* still agrees in gender and number with the noun, e.g. *mucha más lluvia*.

(e) Although the basic rules governing concord of adjectives with nouns of mixed gender and number are fairly straightforward, they need to be learned; and in addition to studying Harmer and Norton's *Manual of Modern Spanish*, for instance, students should consult chapter XXX of Bello and Cuervo's *Gramática* for more detailed rules, as well as for some interesting cases where either of two solutions may be correct.

3. *Proper names*

Where there are established equivalents in Spanish, use them, e.g. *París*. Otherwise it is almost always better to use the English form, e.g. 'Plymouth Hoe' is better left alone!

4. *Adjectives*

(a) Most students of Spanish know that, apart from a few short common adjectives such as *bueno*, the usual position of the adjective is after the noun. However, when the adjective forms part of the noun, or is rather more decorative than distinguishing in function, it tends to precede, e.g. *una mujer hermosa*, but *un hermoso día de junio*. Of course, some adjectives vary in meaning according to their position e.g. *nuevo* preceding the noun means 'fresh'; following the noun it means 'brand new'.

(b) Although the basic rules concerning concord of nouns and adjectives are quite simple and well known, there are a number of complicated cases which arise when nouns of differing gender and number are involved. The student is advised to consult some such work as the Academy Grammar or Bello and Cuervo in case of difficulty; but to be prepared to find that there is no exact parallel to the case with which he is faced.

(c) Remember that in the superlative form of an adjective, the article is not repeated in Spanish, as it is in French, e.g. *el hombre más* (not *el más*) *grande*.

5. *Pronouns*

(a) Although the masculine direct object pronoun is *lo*, *le* is more frequently used when the object is a person, *lo* in these circumstances being considered as a regionalism. Although *le* used as a direct object pronoun to refer to things is not yet accepted in literary usage, it is not uncommon.

(b) It is unnecessary to translate 'it' in sentences like the following: 'I don't think it necessary to do that.' If, as in this case, the 'it' comes before what it refers to, then the translation is *No creo necesario hacerlo*. Cf. 'he knows it all': *todo lo sabe*, where the *lo* follows the word it refers to.

(c) *Sí* is strictly the emphatic reflexive object pronoun, and is used only when the object is the same as the subject, e.g. *se dijo a sí mismo*, 'he told himself'. (There is a common tendency among Spaniards to ignore this rule and say *él*.) *Sí mismo* must never be used when it is the subject of the verb, e.g. *Le dijo que lo hiciera él* (not *sí*) *mismo*.

(d) Remember that with *con* the emphatic reflexive pronoun is not *mí*, *ti*, *sí*, but is combined with the preposition to form *conmigo, contigo, consigo*.

(e) In a case of ambiguity, a Spaniard will presume that *se* has a reflexive meaning rather than any other. Therefore, although the reflexive is frequently used instead of the passive, it is advisable to beware of doing this where personal subjects are concerned: *como si me hubiese encerrado en un armario* will mean to a Spaniard 'shut myself' and not 'been shut'. In this case the indefinite third person plural *como si me hubiesen encerrado* would be preferable if one wished to avoid the passive.

(f) The so-called 'impersonal active *se*' with non-personal reference (cf. English 'one', French *on*, German *man*) is not an accepted literary construction, so that in written Spanish it is advisable to avoid the quite common colloquial expression *se venden botellas*.

(g) The weak demonstrative forms *el que, la que, lo que*, as in the sentence *La que entra es mi mujer*, "The one who is coming in is my wife', is not usual when the demonstrative is followed by a preposition ruling the relative pronoun, e.g. 'The one (i.e. house) in which he lives is the white one' should be *Aquélla* (*casa*) *en que vive es la blanca*, rather than *La en que*, etc., although cases can occur where this rule is ignored.

(h) *Algo* has the function of a noun, and the adjective agrees with it, e.g. *Algo malo va a pasar. Algo de* is used with a noun and indicates a limited amount, e.g. *algo de substancia*. (*Algo* is also of course an adverb, e.g. *Estoy algo cansado*.)

(i) *Poco* and *un poco* mean respectively 'little' and 'a little'. Elementary and obvious, like many of these points, but you'd be surprised how often people forget!

(j) Never use the form *mucho de*: *gran parte de*, or *la mayor parte de* is what is needed in a sentence like 'Much of what you say is true'.

6. *Verbs*

(a) One of the most common stumbling-blocks in Spanish is the use of the gerund, and the student would do well to read Gili y Gaya's helpful section on this subject in the *Curso superior de sintaxis española* (Barcelona, 1961), p. 169 ff. The general rule is that the gerund is used when the action of the verb in the gerund coincides with or immediately precedes in time the main verb of the sentence in which it occurs, as in the example given by Gili y Gaya, *Paseando por el campo, vi aterrizar un avión de pasajeros.* (In the main clause of this sentence, incidentally, it will be noted that the infinitive is used instead of the gerund after a finite verb, where English would have 'landing'). One must not use the gerund in a case where the action indicated follows that of the main verb, as in *El agresor huyó, siendo detenido horas después* (although it is fair to say that it is often done, and indeed is quite acceptable if the action immediately follows that of the main verb, e.g. *Salió cerrando la puerta tras sí*).

The use of the gerund as an attribute is strictly incorrect, as in the example *Era un hombre robusto, alto y gozando de buena salud.* (It is properly used to refer to the subject, as in the following example: *El capitán, viendo que el barco se hundía, mandó preparar las lanchas del salvamento.*) Similarly, although the sentence *Los alumnos, viviendo lejos, llegaban tarde a la escuela*, is correct, since it refers to all the pupils and explains the reason for their lateness (i.e. is adverbial in usage, not adjectival), the same sentence without the commas is incorrect, since *viviendo lejos* does not in that case refer to all the pupils, but has the function of an adjective qualifying *alumnos*, and distinguishing some from others. In such a case one needs to say *Los alumnos que vivían lejos llegaban tarde a la escuela.*

The gerund can refer to the direct complement of the main verb, as in the case *Vi a una muchacha cogiendo manzanas*, the action of the main verb here coinciding temporarily with that of the action of the verb in the gerund; but one cannot use the gerund to refer to a quality or an attribute which is not observably simultaneous with the action of the main verb: hence *Te envío una caja conteniendo libros* is incorrect, and one must say *que contiene*, because the phrase has now become adjectival. In consequence, only verbs indicating sensory or intellectual perception (like *ver, hallar*) or representation (like *pintar, representar*) can take the gerund in this kind of case, e.g. *El autor describe a D. Quijote acometiendo a los molinos de viento.*

(b) Most grammar books contain a good deal of useful information on the differences between perfect, preterite, and imperfect tenses. At the risk of repetition, it is perhaps worth pointing out that the perfect generally refers to actions in the past which have an effect in the present, e.g. *He llegado esta mañana*, 'I arrived this morning (and I am still here),' or even *mi padre ha muerto hace cinco años*; that the preterite refers to things completed in the past, e.g. *Llegué a Londres el año 36 y pasé cinco años en la capital* (i.e. 'it is all over now, and I am no longer there'); and that the imperfect is used to refer to things which happened regularly or habitually in the past, e.g. *Llegaba a la oficina cada lunes a las 9 en punto*, 'I used to arrive, would arrive, was in the habit of arriving, even though I no longer do, and that phase of my life is completely over.'

(c) No attempt will be made here to give any comprehensive account of the use of the subjunctive, to which grammars devote a good deal of attention. However, it is perhaps worth pointing out one conjunction which is *always* followed by the subjunctive, namely *antes que* (or *antes de que*).

(d) If possible, avoid splitting the auxiliary and the participle in compound tenses of the verb. You may find things like *Había sólo dicho* in Old Spanish, but this kind of division of auxiliary and participle is not accepted in modern written Spanish.

(e) The distinction between *ser* and *estar* is notoriously difficult to make correctly, and works on grammar and syntax devote much attention to the problem. For those who know Latin, it might help to remember that *ser* comes from *esse*, which expresses 'essence' or permanent condition; and *estar* from *stare*, which indicates situation or temporary condition. Students of Spanish frequently tie themselves in knots through attempting to apply the rules too rigidly and logically. Perhaps it is a result of experiencing the uncertainties of English weather that we come to think that *ser* is not the verb to use in a sentence like *Era un día puro, alegre, de primavera* (*el día está más bien feo* seems much more natural); but it is worth remembering that, other considerations apart, *estar* is rarely used simply with predicate nouns. *Es soldado* is normal, even though the man in question may be a temporary conscript. *Está de soldado* (note the preposition) would mean that he was making a temporary appearance as a soldier in a play or at a fancy-dress party; or else that he was doing the job of acting as a soldier, etc., e.g. *Está de chófer en casa de mi tío*. Those puzzled by the problems of these two verbs might find it helpful to brood on Gili y Gaya's *Curso superior de sintaxis española*, section 46.

(f) The impersonal form of *haber* is *hay* in the present, whether it refers to singular or plural nouns. Everyone knows this, but when it comes to other tenses there appears to be some doubt among foreigners, and even among less well-educated Spaniards, and one finds all too often the incorrect form *habían* with plural nouns. Incidentally, 'there was' is always translated by *había*, not *estaba*, which must have a definite subject. (*Érase que se era* is a special case used to introduce fairy stories.)

(g) Pronouns must agree in person with their subjects: so, whereas in English one says 'it is I', in Spanish one must say *soy yo*. If you were awkward you might ask how to translate something like this: 'Last night I dreamed I was you', 'you' being, just to make matters more difficult, the familiar second-person form. In this case the agreement would be with 'I' (*que yo era tú*); but if the sentence had been

'Last night I dreamed it was you who came', the translation would be *eras tú*.

7. *Adverbs*

(a) Translation of the English word 'then' proves very difficult. It is never *pues* when referring to time, but only when indicating a consequence, e.g. *Digamos, pues, que Juan es tonto.* The two words normally used for 'then' are *luego* and *entonces*. *Luego* is used in a sequence of events to mean 'next' or 'afterwards', e.g. *Se levantó y luego fue al cuarto de baño*; while *entonces* indicates the end of a series of events, or something completely past, e.g. *Entonces, terminado el trabajo del día, se fue a la cama*; or, *Entonces, en el Siglo de Oro, se escribía una poesía muy distinta de la de hoy.* It will be seen that *entonces* is the only one of the three words discussed that translates 'then' in the sense of 'at that time'.

(b) *Ya* and *todavía* are frequently confused. *Ya* means 'now' or 'already', e.g. *Ya llegó la hora de hacerse soldado*; *todavía* means 'yet' or 'still', e.g. *Todavía no ha llegado*, or *En esta vida moderna todavía existen problemas científicos difíciles de solucionar.* A very common error is *Voy a ver si han llegado todavía*, where Spanish requires *ya* ('I'm going to see if they've arrived yet').

(c) *Aun* and *aún* are also frequently confused. *Aun* means *incluso*, e.g. *Aun dicen que los chinos son más numerosos que todo el resto del mundo*; *aún* means *todavía*, e.g. *Aún se siente enfermo de vez en cuando.* However, in spite of all this, *aun* tends to be used in both senses at the beginning of a phrase, e.g. *Aun no ha llegado*; and *aún* when it follows the word to which it refers, e.g. *No salen aún de clase.* This is quite frankly confusing, and if in doubt it might be better to use *incluso* and *todavía*. Incidentally, it is perhaps worth mentioning that *incluso* means 'even', 'including' being *inclusive*. Cf. *Va incluída la copia que me encargaste.*

(d) *Aquí*, *ahí* and *allí* correspond to the demonstratives *este*, *ese* and *aquel*. M. Seco, in his *Diccionario de dudas de la lengua española*, writes: '*Aquí* es "el sitio donde estoy yo;" *ahí*, "el sitio donde estás tú;" *allí*, "el sitio que está lejos de ti y de mí".'

(e) *Aquí* and *acá*. Seco is again helpful: 'Los dos adverbios designan el lugar donde yo estoy; pero no son completamente sinónimos, ya que el primero lo designa con más precisión que el segundo: *ven aquí* significa "ven a este mismo punto donde yo estoy; ven a mi lado"; *ven acá* significa "ven a esta parte, aproxímate".' The same kind of distinction may be made between *allí* and *allá*: *allá* is much farther away than *allí*. (*Acullá* is farther off still.) Confusion often occurs because Latin American Spanish frequently uses *allá* and *acá* for peninsular *allí* and *aquí*. Incidentally, 'here and there' is normally *acá y allá*.

(f) *A poco, dentro de poco*. Both mean 'shortly afterwards'; but *a poco* refers to the past, and *dentro de poco* to the future.

(g) In translating the relative adverb 'when' in 'the day when', *cuando* is apparently not acceptable in modern Spanish: instead one must use *el día que*, or *en que*.

(h) 'More and more' is *cada vez más*, not *de más en más*.

8. *Prepositions*

These present one of the biggest and most complex problems in any language; and although perhaps not quite so baffling as German, Spanish has plenty of traps for the unwary.

(a) Prepositional links are tricky, and rather than general rules, one is more or less forced to learn particular cases. Most grammars provide lists of verbs followed by certain prepositions with the infinitive, and it is best to learn these by heart. It is *not* safe to assume that things happen in Spanish as they do in French (contrast *je vais manger* with *voy a comer, penser à* with *pensar en*). The preposition *a* is used much less widely in Spanish than in French, and usually, but not always, indicates motion towards something. The logic of the Spanish mind is also somewhat different from that of the English one, preferring *subir a la cama*, whereas we 'climb into bed'. (*Subir en* would indicate rising up when in bed—presumably with it!) Note the formal difference between *recordar* and *acordarse de*.

Equally difficult is the link between some nouns or adjectives and an infinitive (e.g. *propenso a jurar*). The Spanish Academy's *Gramática de la lengua española* 1931 edition has lists (see pages 219, etc.), but one is often disappointed in the search for the precise preposition needed for the particular case one is faced with. For such particular cases, a useful work is María Moliner's *Diccionario de uso del español*.

(b) There is an important difference between a phrase such as *Es fácil leer este libro*, where the infinitive phrase *leer este libro* is the subject of the verb, and no prepositional link is required; and one such as *Este libro es fácil de leer*, where the subject is the noun *este libro*, and the link is between an adjective and an infinitive. (*A*, by the way, is never used in these circumstances.)

(c) Note the (to English ears) tautological use in emphatic sentences in Spanish: *de allí es de donde vengo*; *a quien quiero darlo es a Pedro*; *con quien quería hablar era con el jefe*; and especially *por eso es por lo que lo digo*, an emphatic way of expressing 'that is why I said it'.

(d) The English form of verb of motion + preposition 'to run in' has to be completely recast in Spanish, as, for example, *entrar corriendo*. Of course if the verb has no special significance, one can use a simple verb, e.g. in 'I was having breakfast when Peter walked in', 'walked in' is adequately translated by *entró*.

(e) Remember that *desde* goes with *hasta*, and *de* with *a*. Do not mix these pairs.

(f) The personal *a* gives rise to some knotty problems. How, for instance, is one to translate 'I prefer John to Peter'? In this case it is better to omit the personal *a* and say *Prefiero Juan a Pedro*. On this subject see Bello and Cuervo's *Gramática*, especially section 900 and the whole of their chapter XXXII.

9. *Conjunctions*

(a) *Como* should not be used to translate 'as', if the latter has a temporal value: use *cuando*, *mientras*, or *a medida que*.

(b) *Si* is scarcely ever found with the present subjunctive; with the imperfect subjunctive it is used only if the *si* clause is contrary to fact, e.g. *Si tuviera dinero, compraría la casa*. (Contrast *Si tenía dinero, compraba vino*); or for 'if' clauses of doubtful or unlikely realization, e.g. *Si viniera*, 'If he were to come'.

(c) English 'that' in the following cases is not to be translated as *que*: (i) 'It was there that I saw him' (place) = *Allí fue donde* . . .; (ii) 'It was then that I saw him' (time) = *Entonces fue cuando* . . .; (iii) 'It was thus that I talked to him' (manner) = *Así fue como* . . .

(d) Note the important difference between *la idea que* and *la idea de que*. In the former *que* is a relative pronoun, and refers to the noun itself; in the latter, *de que* is a conjunction, and introduces a noun clause in apposition to the noun *idea*. The following examples will illustrate the distinction: *La idea que has tenido es buena*; *La idea de que me odias/odies me hace rabiar*.

(e) Comparison between two complete clauses, i.e. where two different verbs are involved, as in a case like 'He eats more apples than I can buy', requires not the conjunction *que*, but the conjunctive phrase *del que* (or *de la que*, *de lo que*, *de los que*, *de las que*), e.g. *El come más manzanas de las que yo puedo comprar*; *Es más cruel de lo que crees*. (*Que lo que* is found as an alternative to *de lo que*, etc.)

(f) *Mientras* and *mientras que*, although to some extent interchangeable, correspond to the French *pendant que* and *tandis que*, the former being used in temporal circumstances, the latter to indicate a contrast. Compare *Mientras comía, leía el periódico* and *Mientras que él trabajaba, ella no hacía nada*.

10. Vocabulary

Here the possibilities of error are practically unlimited; and one can only recommend careful study of good dictionaries, including dictionaries of synonyms; as well of course as wide reading of modern Spanish. The following are a few samples from the 'case-book':

(a) *Audiencia* does not mean 'audience' in the usual sense, being a technical term for a judicial hearing. The word required is *auditorio*, or possibly *público*.

(b) *Caber* is an irregular verb, meaning 'to be contained in', or 'to fit in', not 'to contain'. Care must be exercised in its use, e.g. *Estas manzanas apenas caben en la cesta*.

(c) *Deber* and *deber de*+infinitive. The former implies obligation, the latter supposition. Compare *Pedro debe estar en el museo* (i.e. 'is obliged to be') and *Pedro debe de estar en el museo* (i.e. "That's where he'll be").

(d) *Hacerse, ponerse, volverse*+adjective or noun, *Ponerse* is used when the condition indicated by the adjective is less permanent. (Compare *ponerse pálido* and *volverse loco*.) *Hacerse* is more characteristically used with nouns, e.g. *hacerse abogado*. It is worth consulting M. Moliner's *Diccionario de uso del español* on this point; and examples should be learned by heart as they are heard or seen.

(e) *Venir de* is a gallicism for *acabar de*+infinitive, which means 'to have just done something'; use the proper Spanish form. *No acabar de* is not the opposite of *acabar de*: it means 'doesn't quite', e.g. *No me acabó de gustar*.

(f) Spaniards, like other people, are sensitive to jingle; and the avoidance of this may be the deciding factor in choosing between synonyms. Try, for instance, to steer clear of unintentional rhymes and assonances.

Reference Books

Mention has been made in passing of a number of works of reference, which can be broadly divided into dictionaries and books on grammar and syntax.

(a) Dictionaries

There is really no satisfactory bilingual dictionary to be compared for instance with the *Harrap French Dictionary*; and in consequence, more than in the case of other languages, it is necessary as soon as possible to have recourse to an all-Spanish dictionary, of which the best-known is the *Diccionario de la lengua española* of the Real Academia Española, of which the latest edition, the nineteenth, was published in 1970. This is the descendant of the famous *Diccionario de Autoridades*, first published in six volumes between 1726 and 1739, and still an invaluable reference work for the specialist, with its large number of examples. It is treacherous for etymologies, but gives archaisms and dialect forms. Many of the examples are reproduced in the three volumes of Martín Alonso, *Enciclopedia del idioma* (Madrid, 1958); and a recent work on the same lines, but with more emphasis on contemporary usage, is the two-volume *Diccionario de uso del español* of María Moliner (Madrid, 1966–67).

On a more modest level are the *Pequeño Larousse ilustrado* of Miguel de Toro y Gisbert, revised by R. García-Pelayo y Gross, and published in 1964; and *Vox. Diccionario general ilustrado de la lengua española*, edited by Samuel Gili y Gaya (2nd edition, Barcelona, 1953). The former is an encyclopaedia as well as a dictionary.

More specialized dictionaries which will be useful are Julio Casares, *Diccionario ideológico de la lengua española* (2nd edition, Barcelona, 1959), especially for antonyms and for near-synonyms which one can often nearly but not quite recall; the *Duden español. Diccionario por la imagen*, ed. Bibliographisches Institut, Mannheim (London, Harrap, 1963); F. C. Sainz de Robles, *Ensayo de un diccionario español de sinónimos y antónimos* (3rd edition, Madrid, 1953). Other useful dictionaries of synonyms are Roque Barcia, *Sinónimos castellanos* (8th edition, Buenos Aires, 1958); and Santiago Pey and Juan Ruiz Calonja, *Diccionario de sinónimos, ideas afines y contrarios* (Barcelona and London, Harrap, 1966). An invaluable work is Manuel Seco, *Diccionario de dudas y dificultades de la lengua española* (5th edition, Madrid, 1967), which is a kind of Spanish equivalent of Fowler's *Modern English Usage*.

Among the bilingual dictionaries that of A. Cuyás, *Nuevo diccionario Cuyás inglés-español y español-inglés de Appleton*, the latest edition of which was published in New York by Appleton-Century-Crofts in 1966; the *New Revised Velázquez Spanish and English Dictionary* (Chicago and New York, 1967); and that of E. B. Williams (New York, Holt, Rinehart and Winston, 1962), have been found to be the most satisfactory. It is important when using these dictionaries to check the word found in the English–Spanish section in the Spanish–English part, or better still, in an all-Spanish dictionary, to make sure that one has the right word for the situation. (Believe it or not, as an oral examiner I have been told by a candidate, asked what he had been doing before my arrival, that he had been *teniendo un juego de grillo*.)

Those in need of an etymological dictionary should consult Juan Corominas, *Diccionario crítico etimológico de la lengua castellana* (four volumes, Berne, 1954). (The one-volume work by the same author is of very little value.)

One might also mention a work by A. Bryson Gerrard and J. de Heras Heras, called *Beyond the Dictionary in Spanish. A Handbook of Colloquial Usage* (London, Cassell, 1953), a somewhat fuller and more elaborate attempt to do what this introduction aims to achieve. Mr. J. E. Lyon's *Pitfalls in Spanish* (London, Harrap, 1961), is a useful work which students would be well advised to consult. Lastly, for those who want to be up to date on accentuation, reference should be made to the *Nuevas normas de prosodia y ortografía*, (Spanish Academy, revised 1959).

(b) *Grammars, etc.*

It is scarcely necessary to mention L. C. Harmer and F. J. Norton, *A Manual of Modern Spanish*, first published in 1935 by the University Tutorial Press of London, and frequently re-issued. It must be known to all English students who have got beyond the course stage, and is not only invaluable, but, one might venture to say, irreplaceable. Somewhat more specialized works which might complement Harmer and Norton are the *Gramática de la lengua española* of the Spanish Academy (not as reliable as one might expect), first published in 1931, and Andrés Bello's *Gramática de la lengua castellana*, published with R. J. Cuervo's *Notas* in Buenos Aires in 1945.

Works on syntax which are useful for elucidating baffling points are Samuel Gili y Gaya, *Curso superior de sintaxis española* (8th edition, Barcelona, 1961), and Robert K. Spaulding, *Syntax of the Spanish Verb* (New York, 1931). Werner Beinhauer, *El español coloquial*, translated from German by Fernando Huarte, was published in 1963.

Sample Prose Versions

(The first, in each case, by C. A. Jones, the second by a native Spaniard)

Damsels in Distress

The rosy-cheeked, bright-eyed quartet looked so charming in their light summer attire, clinging to the roadside bank like pigeons on a roof-slope, that he stopped a moment to regard them before coming close. Their gauzy skirts had brushed up from the grass innumerable flies and butterflies which, unable to escape, remained caged in the transparent tissue as in an aviary. Angel's eye at last fell upon Tess, the hindmost of the four; she, being full of suppressed laughter at their dilemma, could not help meeting his glance radiantly.

He came beneath them in the water, which did not rise over his long
boots; and stood looking at the entrapped flies and butterflies.

'Are you trying to get to church?', he said to Marian, who was in
front, including the next two in his remark, but avoiding Tess.

'Yes, sir; and 'tis getting late; and my colour do come up so. . . . '

'I'll carry you through the pool—every Jill of you.'

The whole four flushed as if one heart beat through them.

'I think you can't, sir,' said Marian.

'It is the only way for you to get past. Stand still. Nonsense—you are
not too heavy! I'd carry you all four together. Now, Marian, attend,' he
continued, 'and put your arms round my shoulders, so. Now! Hold on.
That's well done.'

Thomas Hardy, Tess of the D'Urbervilles

Muchachas en un apuro

Las cuatro muchachas con sus mejillas rosadas y sus ojos brillantes
tenían un aspecto tan encantador, con su ligero traje de verano, pegán-
dose al margen de la carretera como palomas en un tejado inclinado,
que se paró él un momento a contemplarlas antes de acercarse. Sus
faldas diáfanas habían ido recogiendo de la hierba innumerables moscas
y mariposas las cuales, no pudiendo escaparse, quedaban enjauladas en
la tela transparente como en una pajarera. Por fin la mirada de Ángel
cayó sobre Tess, la última de las cuatro; ella, reprimiendo su risa ante
el dilema de ellas, no pudo menos de encontrar su mirada, radiante.

Pasó debajo de ellas por el agua, que no se alzaba lo suficiente para
cubrir sus altas botas; y quedó mirando las moscas y mariposas atrapadas.

'¿Pensáis llegar a la iglesia?', dijo a Mariana, que iba delante,
incluyendo en su pregunta a las que seguían, pero sin dirigirse a Tess.

'Sí, señor; y se va haciendo tarde; y se me sube tanto el color...'

'Os llevaré a través del charco — a cada una de vosotras.'

Todas las cuatro se ruborizaron como si un solo corazón latiese en
ellas.

'No creo que pueda', dijo Mariana.

'Es el único modo de que podáis pasar. No os mováis. ¡Disparate —
no pesáis demasiado! Os llevaría a todas las cuatro juntas. Ahora,
Mariana, ¡atención!' prosiguió, 'y pon los brazos alrededor de mis
hombros, así. ¡Ahora! ¡Agárrate! Perfectamente.'

El cuarteto tenía un aspecto tan encantador, todas con sus ligeros
trajes de verano, las mejillas color rosa, los ojos claros, y pegadas al
declive del borde de la carretera como palomas en la pendiente de un

tejado, que él se paró un momento para mirarlas antes de acercarse. Sus faldas como de gasa habían arrancado de la hierba innumerables moscas y mariposas que, al no poderse escapar, quedaron enjauladas en el transparente tejido como si estuvieran en una pajarera. Por fin la mirada de Ángel fue a parar a Tess, la última de las cuatro, la cual, muerta de risa que se estaba conteniendo ante el dilema que se les presentaba, no pudo por menos de cruzar con él su rápida mirada de manera radiante.

Ángel se acercó por debajo de ellas caminando por el agua que no le subía por encima de sus botas altas, y se quedó mirando a las atrapadas moscas y mariposas.

'¿Es que quieren Vds. ir a la iglesia?', dijo a Marian que estaba en frente, incluyendo en esta observación a las otras dos que estaban a su lado., pero evitando a Tess.

'Sí, señor, y se está haciendo tarde. Y a mí se me suben tanto los colores...'

'Yo les pasaré el charco... a todas'.

Las cuatro se pusieron coloradas como si un solo corazón latiera por todas.

'Creo que no podrá Vd.', dijo Marian.

'Esa es la única manera de que puedan pasar. Quédense donde están. ¡Qué tontería! No pesan Vds. tanto. Las podría pasar a las cuatro juntas. Ahora fíjese, Marian,' siguió diciendo, 'y cójame por los hombros con los brazos. Así. ¡Venga! Agárrese bien. Eso es, así.'

American Patriarchal Customs

When Helena, who was always the last down, had finished her breakfast, the coloured maid would bring in a big china basin with pretty roses on it and a pitcher full of hot water, and Mrs. Davison would wash the breakfast cups and saucers at the table (an old pioneer custom, she said) and dry them on an embroidered tea towel. At dinner, after the main course, the maid would bring in a salad bowl of Chinese porcelain, red and green, and an old cruet stand with olive oil, a mustard pot, and vials of different kinds of vinegar, and Mr. Davison, standing up, would make the salad dressing himself and mix the salad, which was always sprinkled with fresh herbs. They did not entertain very often; most of the family friends, Kay said, were rather old, bachelors or widows, and neither Mr. Davison (whose real name was Edward) nor Mrs. Davison was enthusiastic about what they humorously called 'followers', though Helena, being an only child, had been given *every opportunity* at her progressive day school to meet boys and girls of her own age. Not to mention dancing school and Sunday school; neither Mr. Davison nor Mrs. Davison was a regular churchgoer (although Mrs. Davison was a sharp judge of a sermon), but they felt it only right that Helena should know the Bible and the beliefs of the principal Christian creeds, so that she could make up her own mind.

Mary McCarthy, *The Group*

Costumbres patriarcales americanas

Cuando Elena, que era siempre la última en bajar, había terminado el desayuno, la criada negra traía una gran jofaina de cerámica con lindas rosas pintadas en ella, y una jarra de agua caliente; y la Señora Davison lavaba las tazas y los platillos del desayuno en la mesa (vieja costumbre de los colonizadores, según decía ella), y los enjugaba con un paño bordado. En la cena después del plato principal, la criada traía una ensaladera de porcelana china, roja y verde, y unas viejas vinagreras con aceite de oliva, una mostacera, y frascos con diferentes especies de vinagre; y el Señor Davison, de pie, preparaba la salsa él mismo y aliñaba la ensalada, que iba siempre condimentada con hierbas frescas. No recibían huéspedes con mucha frecuencia; la mayor parte de los amigos de la familia, decía Kay, eran bastante viejos, solteros o viudos, y ni el Señor Davison (cuyo verdadero nombre era Eduardo) ni la Señora Davison, se entusiasmaban mucho por los que llamaban de manera humorística moscones, aunque Elena, siendo hija única, había recibido toda oportunidad en su progresivo externado de conocer a muchachos y muchachas de su propia edad, sin mencionar la esuela de baile y la escuela de domingo; ni el Señor Davison ni la Señora Davison iban muy frecuentemente a la iglesia (aunque la Señora Davison sabía juzgar un sermón con agudeza), pero sentían que era justo que Elena conociera la Biblia y las creencias de las principales sectas cristianas, para que pudiera formar sus propias opiniones.

Cuando Elena, que era siempre la última en bajar, terminaba el desayuno, la criada negra traía una gran fuente de china en la que había rosas preciosas y un jarro lleno de agua caliente, y entonces la Sra. Davison fregaba las tazas y los platos del desayuno en la mesa y los secaba con un paño de cocina bordado. Ella decía que esto era una vieja costumbre de los pioneros. En la cena, después del plato fuerte, la criada traía una fuente de porcelana de china roja y verde, y unas viejas vinagreras con aceite de oliva, un cacharrito de mostaza y unos frasquitos de distintas clases de vinagre. Entonces el Sr. Davison, poniéndose de pie, hacía la ensalada, a la que siempre se rociaba con hierbas frescas, aliñándole y dándole vueltas él mismo. No recibían con mucha frecuencia. Kay decía que la mayor parte de los amigos de la familia eran bastante viejos: solterones o viudas, y ni el Sr. Davison (cuyo verdadero nombre era Eduardo) ni la Sra. Davison manifestaban mucho entusiasmo por los que ellos llamaban de manera humorística 'los moscones', aunque a Elena, como era hija única, le habían dado *todas las oportunidades* en su avanzada escuela de externos para que conociese a chicos y a chicas de su edad. Aparte de la escuela parroquial de baile y de la cataquesis de los domingos, ni el Sr. ni la Sra. Davison iban a la iglesia con regularidad, aunque la Sra. Davison sabía juzgar un sermón con agudeza, pero les parecía que al menos era apropiado que Elena conociese la Biblia y las creencias de los principales credos cristianos para que pudiese decidir por ella misma.

Section 1. NARRATIVE

*1. The Bus Stop**

A few minutes later Dixon, carrying a small suitcase, was hurrying through the streets to his bus stop. At the corner of the main road he had a view downhill to where the last few terraced houses and small provisions shops began to give place to office blocks, the more fashionable dress shops and tailors, the public library, the telephone exchange, and a modern cinema. Beyond these again were the taller buildings of the city centre with its tapering cathedral spire. Trolley-buses hummed or ground their way towards it and away from it, with columns of cars winding, straightening, contracting, and thinning out. The pavements were crowded. As Dixon crossed the road, the sight of all this energy made his spirits lift, and somewhere behind his thoughts an inexplicable excitement stirred. There was no reason to suppose that the week-end would contain anything better than the familiar mixture of predicted boredom with unpredicted boredom, but for the moment he was unable to believe this. The acceptance of his article might be the prelude to a run of badly needed luck. He was going to meet some people who might prove interesting and amusing. If not, then he and Margaret could relish talking about them. He must see that she enjoyed herself as far as possible, and doing this would be easier in the presence of others.

Kingsley Amis, *Lucky Jim*

*2. The New Property***

They stood and smiled at each other. Pilon noticed that the worry of property was settling on Danny's face. No more in life would that face be free of care. No more would Danny break windows now that he had windows of his own to break. Pilon had been right—he had been raised among his fellows. His shoulders had strengthened to withstand the

complexity of life. But one cry of pain escaped him before he left for all
time his old and simple existence.

'Pilon', he said sadly, 'I wish you owned it and I could come to
live with you.'

While Danny went to Monterey to have the water turned on, Pilon
wandered into the weed-tangled back yard. Fruit trees were there bony
and black with age, and gnarled and broken from neglect. A few tent-
like chicken coops lay amongst the weeds. A pile of rusty barrel hoops,
a heap of ashes and a sodden mattress. Pilon looked over the fence into
Mrs. Morales' chicken yard, and after a moment of consideration he
opened a few small holes in the fence for the hens. 'They will like to
make nests in the tall weeds' he thought kindly. He considered how he
could make a figure-four trap in case the roosters came in too and
bothered the hens and kept them from the nests. 'We will live happily,'
he thought again.

John Steinbeck, Tortilla Flat

3. The Neighbouring Farm**

Elijah had gone that morning to buy heifers at a neighbouring farm, and
the kitchen told Luke to come back again in the early evening. When he
walked across the fields again in the cold clear twilight the wind was
dropping, but the furrows in the ploughed lands were bleached white
on the eastern side, and in the cornfields the young flourishing shoots of
winter wheat lay flattened against the earth by the cold wind as though
by a roller. All about the big stone farmhouse the damson trees, very
old and uncoloured yet by the blossom buds, stood out black against
the wind-cleared sky. When he arrived at the farm the hands had
knocked off, the hens were cooped up for the night, and there was a
strange evening silence everywhere. Then when the kitchen girl opened
the door to him she put her hand up to her mouth in half-frightened
fashion. The family were at evening prayers.

He stood in the half-dark passage running from the kitchen door to
the parlour and waited for them to finish. The young girl, nervous and
silent, waited at his side. They stood together without exchanging a word
until the last words of the last prayer had been spoken. He could hear at
first two thin uncertainly upraised soprano voices joined together by the
harmony of Thompson's bass, then the solitary voice of Thompson
reading the scripture, and, finally the repetition of the benedictory
prayer. It reminded him of his mother and of his childhood. When the

sounds ceased at last the girl knocked at the door. Thompson called for it to be opened. The girl, as though scared by the voice gave the wooden knob a single jerk, and scurried back along the passage, leaving him there alone, slightly apprehensive and not knowing what to do, until Thompson called out;

'Well, well, whoever it is, come in, come in.'

H. E. Bates, *The Poacher*

4. A Long, Hot Day***

As dawn broke, the Ballantyne kids arrived and watched the stockmen boiling tea and washing their white hairy chests in blackened half petrol-tin dixies. Then they ran helter-skelter over the ground, enacting on foot among the flags the events of horsemanship that soon were to take place. Meanwhile the sun rose implacably as it did all through the Ballantyne summer, regularly as clockwork, never muted by a cloud, and only gentle in the tepid dawn and in the slow late twilight. It lit up the main road that is all Ballantyne consists of with a determined hard glare; the metalled strip in the middle and the wide tracts of baked clay on either side which you cross to reach the stores, Willy Matthew's bank, the post office, or the liquor Palace. From an early hour the cars and horses came up this road at either end of the township, raising the dust to a steady hanging cloud that spread from the railway station to the Recreational ground itself.

Some families came in by rail from halts down the line where they'd flagged the night train from the capital that reaches Ballantyne about ten. The train waits reluctantly for just a few minutes, shivering and steaming, while the tousled passengers walk up and down the cinders spitting, and swarm into the buffet for cups of tea. Arthur Wesley, carrying no luggage, got last off the train, hunched up his shoulders and strolled past the end of the platform into the wilderness of lines and sheds beyond it that stink of greasy wool.

Colin MacInnes, *June in Her Spring*

5. Response to Pictures*

Norah Palmer responded easily and certainly to pictures. Response was more difficult for Peter Ash; it worried him. In spite of his great responsibility as host of the Living Arts (perhaps because of it), he was

3—A.S.P.C.

timid in aesthetic judgment. Perhaps if he had been to a university, it might have been easier for him; he had always been a great reader, but that was not the same. He listened to Norah Palmer, and envied the easy superficiality of her judgments. She took these things for granted, he thought, because she had been to Cambridge, and just—just connecting with pictures was not a problem for her; she had accepted them like breathing. He did not talk to her of his difficulty in connecting. Even after nine years, more than ever after nine years—he could not do that. More and more as time sets a relationship into habit, there are secret places, little areas of personal privacy, that one guards against discovery. If in the course of their life together, Norah Palmer were to blunder into one of these places (and it happened sometimes), Peter Ash would feel relieved. Opened up, the place might not seem secret and shameful at all. Until that happened, he kept silent. He was afraid of mockery. His trouble was, you see, that he felt nothing.

John Bowen, The Birdcage

6. *Ambition**

Why had he never used his powers? Why had he done nothing? Sometimes I thought he was too proud to compete—and also too diffident. Perhaps at the deepest level pride and diffidence became the same. He could not risk a failure. He was born to be admired from below, but he could not bear the rough and tumble, the shame, the breath of the critics. His pride was mountainous, his diffidence intense. Even that night he had been forced to clown before he scarified his enemies. He despised what others said of him, and yet could not endure it.

There was one other thing. Through pride, through diffidence, he had spent his life among men whose attention he captured without an effort, with whom he did not have to compete. But it was the final humiliation if they would not recognize him. That was why the Mastership lived in his mind like an obsession. He ought to have been engaged in a struggle for great power; he blamed himself that he was not, but it sharpened every desire of his for this miniature power. He ought to have been just Paul Jago, known to all the world with no title to describe him, his name more glowing than any title. But his nature had forced him to live all his life in the college; at least, he must be Master of it.

C. P. Snow, The Masters

7. *The Holy Man***

Even Narouz shuddered as he gazed upon that ravaged face, the eyes of which had been painted with crayon so that they looked glaring, in-human, like the eyes of a monster in a cartoon. The holy man hurled oaths and imprecations at the circle of listeners, his fingers curling and uncurling into claws as he worked upon them, dancing this way and that like a bear at bay, turning and twirling, advancing and retreating upon the crowd with grunts and roars and screams until it trembled before him, fascinated by his powers. He had 'come already into his hour', as the Arabs say, and the power of the spirit had filled him.

The holy man stood in an island of the fallen bodies of those he had hypnotized, some crawling about like scorpions, some screaming or bleating like goats, some braying. From time to time he would leap upon one of them uttering hideous screams and ride him across the ring, thrashing at his buttocks like a maniac, and then suddenly turning, with the foam bursting from between his teeth, he would dart into the crowd and pick up some unfortunate victim, shouting; 'Are you mocking me?' and catching him by his nose or an ear or an arm, drag him with inhuman force into the ring where with a sudden quick pass of his talons he would 'kill his light' and hurl him down among the victims already crawling about in the sand at his feet, to utter shrill cries for mercy which were snuffed out by the braying and hooting of those already under his spell. One felt the power of his personality shooting out into the tense crowd like sparks from an anvil.

Lawrence Durrell, Balthazar

8. *Absconding**

You never get used to absconding. I remember once we went for sixty-one days without an absconder; there were six hundred boys in the reformatory, and nearly half of them could have walked away at any time. Day after day went by of peace unbroken except for trifling offences, and you couldn't help being proud of it, though you kept your pride secret so that no hand out of the sky could strike you down for presumption. Then on the sixty-second day a boy ran away, and we were as downcast as though the sixty-one days had never happened. Somehow you never got used to it.

A time of heavy absconding was a trial of the soul. You felt as though the whole institution was cracking and breaking; you felt you were inefficient, a bungler, a theorist who had theories but no knowledge of human nature; you felt judged even by your own staff and your own boys. And you feared too, although you didn't talk about it, that some newspaper would get hold of it, and print in some careless corner the words that would bring your career to an end, and kill the faith in your heart that your way was the right way, and make you nothing in the eyes of the world and your wife and your children. For the Principal of a great institution has almost divine powers, and is admired by his friends and family.

Alan Paton, Debbie Go Home

9. *The Barrier***

As always, too, he found himself wishing to know them better, and learn more of them. It was not for lack of trying he had made so little headway. He had tried patiently and persistently, ever since they were small. They accepted him as much as they accepted anyone, and he, for his part, probably understood them quite as well as, if not better than, any of their mentors at The Grange. Superficially they were friendly with him—which they were not with many—they were willing to talk with him, and to listen, to be amused, and to learn; but it never went further than the superficial, and he had a feeling that it never would. Always, quite close under the surface, there was a barrier. What he saw and heard from them was their adaptation to their circumstances; their true selves and real nature lay beneath the barrier. Such understanding as passed between himself and them was curiously partial and impersonal; it lacked the dimension of feeling and sympathy. Their real lives seemed to be lived in a world of their own, as shut off from the main current as any Amazonian tribe with its utterly different standards and ethics. They were interested, they learnt, but one had the feeling that they were simply collecting knowledge—somewhat, perhaps, as a juggler acquires a useful skill which, however he may excel with it, has no influence whatever upon him, as a person. Zellaby wondered if anyone would get close to them. The people up at The Grange were an unforthcoming lot, but, from what he had been able to discover, even the most assiduous had been held back by the same barrier.

John Wyndham, The Midwich Cuckoos

10. Robo-Drive*

He marvelled at the electronic brain—actually, he suspected, a quite simple device—which kept the car unswervingly on its path and regulated its speed at every turn. As the clerk had explained, and as he could now see for himself, the whole system of robo-drive depended on clusters of slim, needlelike beams of light which cut across the highway at regular intervals just a few inches from the pavement, emanating from squat mounds of concrete placed alongside the road. On the right-hand side of the car there was a photoelectric-cell mechanism which intercepted these rays and transmitted their messages to the robot brain, so that actually the robot was receiving instructions on how to drive the car every few hundred feet. It was these rays which told the automatic driver when it was deviating a few inches to the left or right; when it was slackening off a couple of miles or infinitesimally picking up speed; when there was another car in the same lane up ahead, or when there was a curve coming and what the speed should be reduced to to negotiate it safely; when it was safe to accelerate again.

Bernard Wolfe, *Limbo '90*

11. Mars***

When Camillo had despatched that message, he swung the transmitter across on its bracket to lock it safely against the wall, and then lay back on his couch. Raul and I were already in position on ours. My work was finished and I had nothing to do but wait. Raul had the extension control panel clamped across his couch in a position where he would still be able to operate it against a pressure of several gravities, if necessary. Everything had gone according to expectations except that our outer surface temperature was somewhat higher than had been calculated—suggesting that the atmosphere is a trifle denser than has been assumed —but the error was small, and of little practical significance.

Raul set about adjusting the angle of the ship, tilting her to preserve the inclination in relation to the braking thrust as we slowed. Our couches turned on their gimbals as the speed decreased and the braking thrust of the main tubes became our main support. Finally, when the speed was virtually zero, and we were standing balanced on our discharge, his job, too, was over. He switched in the landing control. and lay back, watching the progress of our descent, on the dials.

Beneath us, there now splayed downwards eight narrow radar beams matched for proximity, and each controlling a small lateral firing tube. The least degree of tilt was registered by one or more of the beams, and corrected by a short blast which restored the ship to balance on the point of the main drive. Another beam directed vertically downwards controlled the force of the main drive itself, relating it to the distance of the surface below, and thus regulating the speed of descent.

John Wyndham and Lucas Parkes, The Outward Urge

12. A Scugnizzo**

'Now! Now, I will show you how a scugnizzo is made. The foundation of his normal life is destroyed. He must build another for himself. He becomes vain and boastful, because there is no love to affirm his real value as a son of a family, as a son of God. He becomes cunning, because there is no love to protect him from the malice of others. There is only himself, the animal. He cheats and lies because honesty would make him the prey of those who have no love in their heart. He becomes nervous, raucous, unstable, because his child's body cannot keep pace with his explosive psychological development. His body becomes stunted as you have seen, while his mind spreads itself in rank and twisted growth like a weed on a dunghill. Sometimes he is a little mad. Sometimes . . .' Borrelli's face darkened. 'Sometimes the burden of life becomes too much for him and he commits suicide.'

He put his hands up to his face and pressed the palms into his eyeballs as if to blot out a terrifying vision. Then he calmed a little and went on;

'When I went on the streets, I was a man. More than this, I was a priest with years of discipline and study behind me. But I tell you, truly, even I was affected by this naked, loveless existence. When I stood outside the tourist hotel and pleaded to carry a bag, I hated the well-fed smiling men and the women whose clothes would feed a scugnizzo for more than a year. When I saw the police with their truncheons and their little black pistols, I wanted to spit on them and hammer their faces with my fists. Could they not see our wretchedness? Were we not human as they were? What right had they to thrust us out of their way as if we were animals and they a special creation of the Almighty?'

Morris West, Children of the Sun

13. Cabbage*

I must say that the evidence satisfies that that was the sort of dinner this hotel de luxe par excellence supplied. I think, too, that when the plaintiff said: 'A hot waitress steamed across the room hissing, "thick clear or sardine",' I was given a fair idea of what the plaintiff had to endure. Only on one point do I find against the plaintiff in this connexion. He complains that cabbage was served and that it was a soggy mess. I quite agree with the plaintiff that that might be a ground for complaint. But, having regard to the fact that that is the normal way of dealing with that delicious vegetable, even in restaurants of acknowledged excellence, I cannot hold that against the defendants. I do not think that their cabbage, almost tasteless and ruined as it was, was any worse than that which is normally supplied, up and down the country, by cooks and chefs of every description. I regret to say that the same abominable treatment of cabbage takes place in many homes, too. That what was served to the plaintiff was a soggy mess, I accept, but that apparently is all the Englishman expects of cabbage, even in the most exclusive restaurants and clubs.

Henry Cecil, *Sober as a Judge*

14. The Flat**

In winter Marcus's flat, though not actually cold, became blackened and frost-bitten. Perhaps the electric bulbs were not strong enough. Often as the evening settled, he would ring up his parents and invite himself to dinner with them, and then drive out through the dusk to their enormous house, near Ken Wood. It seemed hardly smaller than Ken Wood itself; but it was fake Tudor. It had fifteen rooms and a tennis court. Marcus would run his car off the gravelled drive into the laurel bushes, so as to leave room for his father's much larger car to get to the garage. There was always some orange light showing through the curtains, at the low latticed casement windows at the front of the house; and an iron framed lantern with red, faceted glass hung in the tiled porch. Marcus still had his own latch-key. As he let himself into the hall, he always welcomed the warmth, even though the central heating had an oily smell. But he could not welcome or feel welcomed by the red-tiled floor, the oaken settle whose seat lifted to reveal a chest, where no one needed to keep anything, or the discreet door, almost disguised as part of the wall, of the downstairs lavatory. It was all hideous.

It was home, it was meant to make him comfortable, and it was over-furnished; yet it was empty. Everything removed itself, vacated space, asserted nothing . . . it was too willing to accommodate him.

Brigid Brophy, Flesh

15. On Westminster Bridge**

She took her hand off the wall, and turned. The bridge was as empty as the river; no vehicles or pedestrians here, no craft there. In all that City she might have been the only living thing. She had been so impressed by the sense of security and peace while she had been looking down at the river that only now did she begin to try and remember why she was there on the bridge. There was a confused sense in her mind that she was on her way somewhere; she was either going to or coming from her own flat. It might have been to meet Richard, though she had an idea that Richard, or someone with Richard, had told her not to come. But she could not think of anyone, except Richard, who was at all likely to do so, and anyhow she knew she had been determined to come. It was all mixed up with that crash which had put everything out of her head; and as she lifted her eyes, she saw beyond the Houses and the Abbey the cause of the crash, the plane lying half in the river and half on the Embankment. She looked at it with a sense of its importance to her, but she could not tell why it should seem so important. Her only immediate concern with it seemed to be that it might have blocked the direct road home to her flat, which lay beyond Millbank and was where Richard was or would be and her own chief affairs.

Charles Williams, All Hallows' Eve

Section 2. DESCRIPTIVE

16. The Vestibule**

We went out at the French doors and along a smooth red-flagged path that skirted the far side of the lawn from the garage. The boyish-looking chauffeur had a big black and chromium sedan out now and was dusting that. The path took us along to the side of the greenhouse and the butler opened a door for me and stood aside. It opened into a sort of vestibule that was about as warm as a slow oven. He came in after me, shut the outer door, opened an inner door and we went through that. Then it was really hot. The air was thick, wet, steamy and larded with the cloying smell of tropical orchids in bloom. The glass walls and roof were heavily misted and big drops of moisture dropped down on the plants. The light had an unreal greenish colour, like light filtered through an aquarium tank. The plants filled the place, a forest of them, with nasty leaves and stalks like the newly washed fingers of dead men. They smelled as overpowering as boiling alcohol under a blanket.

The butler did his best to get me through without being smacked in the face by the sodden leaves, and after a while we came to a clearing in the middle of the jungle, under the domed roof.

Raymond Chandler, *The Big Sleep*

17. The Old Town*

The medley of tobacconists and second rate pubs huddled round the station soon gave place to a rather dreary street of small villas; and this in turn to the squalid, beautiful houses of the old town. A little beyond the boundary of these two worlds they turned off to the right, and shortly arrived at the wrought-iron gates of the clergy-house, which had been built in the eighteenth century to replace the old clergy-house adjoining the north transept; this being now used for storing lumber, holding choir practices, and other miscellaneous and untidy purposes. The gates, suspended on either side from pillars of soft, lemon-coloured stone, opened upon a depressing vista of shrubs and lawns, bisected by an overgrown gravel drive which curved round to the front door, skirted the house, and led out beyond the extensive kitchen-gardens on to the cathedral hill itself. Geoffrey entered these regions with circumspection, peering intently at a withered laurel as though he expected it to contain springs, nets and line for his discomfort.

In this realm of celibacy, the first thing they heard was a girl's voice. 'Josephine!' it called, then with more force, and a tinge of irritation; 'Come back!'

Edmund Crispin, Holy Disorders

18. Ávila***

Eighty-six towers and nine gates of glowing bronze! What vivid blazonry of history was this which the July sun made of the walls of Ávila? For an hour this untouchable and terrible city flamed against the sky. Then the sun sank and the patient granite walls were pale again in the lowering evening. Ávila became once more the turreted imagination of antique parchment missals, more mediaeval than her history and less real; the heraldic emblem, the citadel of Castile and of ancient Catholic Spain. From the distant plain, shining in the delicate upland summer, the fortifications of Ávila gleam, as visionary as the retreating towers of romance. Then they become unapproachable cliffs with golden seas flooding to their base. Close beneath, the unpeopled towers guard a searching silence, their sentries the storks motionless on the gates and belfries, their men-at-arms the swallows, their flying arrows the blue darts of myriad and living wings. From the cross on the opposite hill the mass of her climbing towers is so formidable that it is hard to believe any town ever needed such a defence. They remain now symbol and monument of the great dead of Ávila. High on their turrets the storks stand in delicate silhouette against the sky, immovable, like the devices on a coat of arms. Every year, and always on the day of San Blas, one or two appear on the towers, to fly when the harvest is reaped, like the fireflies in Tuscany, watchmen, it would seem of the green and growing corn.

Gertrude and Muirhead Bone, Days In Old Spain

19. The Villa***

There were rooms on the ground floor containing four wardrobes, one
for each wall; there were others with whole battle lines of tables, great
and small; yet others were crammed with cabinets, brackets, and minor
knick-knacks. In the overcrowded living-rooms on the second floor
there were mirrors of all sizes and over ornate frames and green reflections. In the bedrooms there were two, three and even four beds
ranged side by side, as in a hospital. The lobbies and passages were
cluttered up with marble torsos, chests and pieces of armour; on the
walls were huge blackening seventeenth-century pictures; by the staircase hung a series of pale tapestries with a whole population of soft and
shadowy figures. Everything was dark, dank, creaking and shadowy.
The feeling of the sea never penetrated; nor the radiant light of the
coast; for the antique dealer had put some of his pieces of stained glass
into the windows, for want of a better place. A musty, tomb-like smell
of old wood, mould and mice hovered in those air-tight rooms, and the
furniture with its strange arbitrary arrangement seemed to rebuff
human intrusion with surly self-sufficiency. For Tancredi's mother the
house was uncomfortable—impossible to keep it clean, impossible to
move about without knocking into something—and, as she was saying,
not without complacency, it was a great responsibility living in such a
museum, for it would be a disaster if anything got broken. But for
Tancredi, given his inclinations, it was worse than uncomfortable; it
was terrifying; though not without that background of delicious
anguish that fear inspires when it ceases to be a normal state and
becomes the rule.

Alberto Moravia, *Bitter Honeymoon*

20. Summer Days*

On summer days like this in harvest, the richness of the ground seems
charged upon the air, so that even the blue of the sky is tainted like the
water of a cow pond, enriched but no longer pure. It is as if a thousand
years of cultivation have brought to all, trees, grass, crops, even the sky
and the sun, a special quality belonging only to very old countries. A
quality not of matter only, but of thought; as if the hand that planted
the trees in their chosen places had imposed upon them the dignity of
beauty appointed; but taken from them, at the same time, the innocence
of natural freedom. As if the young farmer who set the hedge, to divide

off his inheritance, wrote with its crooked line the history of human growth of responsibility not belonging to the wild hawthorn, but to human love and fatherhood; as if upon the wheat lay the colour of harvest since Alfred, and its ears grew plump with the hopes and anxieties of all those generations that sowed with Beowulf and ploughed with Piers and reaped with Cobbett. Even at my own last harvest at Tolbrook, nine years ago, the gardener's boy brought me from the field a little plait of straw. He did not know what it was or why he brought it, or that he was repeating a sacrifice to the corn god made so long ago that it was thousands of years old when Alfred was the modern man in a changing world.

Joyce Cary, To Be A Pilgrim

21. Earlsdon Central***

Earlsdon Central was the hub of the borough. From it, like the spokes of a wheel, the main roads diverged; the Appian Way was on your left as you came out of the station and led down past the new flats there had been so much fuss about—the Tory majority on the Earlsdon council feared they would bring Labour voters to the district—and ultimately petered out in the back streets of Finchley; the Earlsdon Way ran at right angles to the Appian Way and Edward followed the straggle of bowler-hatted business-men who turned right and then right again in order to follow it on its march towards the promised, yet always distant, countryside. Earlsdon Central itself was a great almond ring of fawn brick shops and chain-stores; Woolworth's, the Co-op, Smith's, Sainsbury's, the A.B.C.; and interspersed between their local rivals—Higgins the greengrocer; Maison Delarge (prop. Mortimer Hague), hair saloon; Crisp, confectioner and newsagent; and the rest. The core of the circle was a grass-topped roundabout with tall concrete lamp standards, each with a double sodium fitting. 'Keep left' signs greeted incoming motorists. The insignia of the Borough of Earlsdon were depicted in coloured pebbles on the top of the roundabout where they could be seen only from the upper deck of a bus. Trolley-bus lines were strung away down Coronation Road towards Michael's corner and there was a trolley around in the western segment of the roundabout. Extra poles, painted light blue, bearing the E.B.C. crest, held up the necessary wires. On the pavement were additional concrete sodium lamps of a slightly different design which bathed the hoop of shops in orange light throughout the endless evenings; it was never night in Earlsdon.

Frederick Raphael, The Earlsdon Way

22. Fishing***

She rowed a little farther until she could no longer see the mill beyond the high bend of the stream, and then tied up the boat on the right bank, under a line of willows. Two hundred yards upstream was an iron bridge built into concrete supports, into a single span on which, in the early days of the occupation, a sentry had waited to halt the farm traffic that never came. Now the Germans had taken him away.

She tied the boat up to the branch of a willow and began to fit together the two sections of rod. The whole rod was about fourteen feet long. She threaded about thirty feet of line through the rings and then tied it, without a reel, to the thicker end. She had made a float from a goose-quill, and she fixed that, with a rather large hook, to the free end of the line. She nicked a worm on the end of the hook and then swung the line, in a low cast, across the stream. When the float stood straight the flow of the stream took it away to the full curve of the line so that it circled down beyond the bows of the boat and back again until it rested just clear of a ring of lily leaves. The girl tightened the line and rested the rod in a rowlock of the boat.

The sun had fallen quite rapidly in the time it had taken her to row up the river, and now the light was falling so that the roots of the willow, now in shade, were losing their look of scarlet hair. They flowed with the motion of the stream like tawny strands of seaweed, darkening every time the girl looked into the depths of the stream.

H. E. Bates, *Fair Stood the Wind for France*

23. Revolution***

A string of dull bumps now, from many quarters at once—as of small geological faults opening in the earth somewhere along the battlements of the fortress. We ran down the steps and along the unlit gravel road to where the main road joined it. A few bewildered-looking civilians stood dazed in the shadows of the trees. 'Over there', said a man. He pointed in the direction of the Secretariat building which was about two hundred yards down the road. The street lamps were so few that we ran in and out of pools of darkness on the fringes of the unpavemented highway. We came round the last corner abreast and walked into a wall of solid yellow fog smelling strongly of something—cordite? In the vagueness figures walked about, aimlessly, with detached curiosity, uncertain whether to go or to stay. They did not seem to have any more business than we did. There was a tidy rent in the wall of the Secretariat out of which smoke poured as if from a steam engine. 'Dust', said my brother grimly, 'from under the administrators' chairs.' But there was no time for jests; somewhere a siren began to wail in the direction of the Wrens' headquarters. A lorry load of police materialized vaguely out of the yellow coils of fog. And then another series of isolated bangs and, after an interval, a deeper growl which was followed by a sudden small contortion of the still night air. 'The whole bloody issue is going up', said my brother fretfully; he had been peevish all evening about the failure of his film which had run into difficulties, he said, due to a sudden wave of non-co-operation which followed hard upon a visit by the parish priest to his actors. 'Wherever I go there's a bloody revolution.' He had just come back from Paraguay where they had revolted under him, so to speak. A bang near at hand lent wings to our purpose. 'I must get back to my animals,' he said. 'The owls have to be fed.'

Lawrence Durrell, Bitter Lemons

24. The Piebald**

They reached a field not far away, enclosed by a stone wall, and Velvet changed the saddle and bridle, tying Sir Pericles with the halter to the gate. She mounted the piebald, and walked and trotted him quietly in large circles. His mouth was a mixture of lead and rubber. He had no notion how to obey the bit but imagined that to turn his head was all that was wanted. He would trot onwards with his neck turned to one side like a horse that has no face. Velvet had to rock him with her knees to get him out of his orbit, and even then it was no more than a be-wildered stagger to one side. She set him to canter. It was clumsy and gallant, and accomplished with snorts. He flung his powerful white head up into the air and nearly smashed his rider's precious plate. Sir Pericles watched. The flashing piebald snorted excitedly round the field. Above him sat the noble child, thin as famine, bony as a Roman, aquiline nose and domed white forehead, tufted loonily with her cotton hair. Velvet, with her great teeth and parted lips, her eye sockets and the pale eyes in them, looked like a child model for a head of Death, an eager bold young death. She was thinking of something far outside the field. She was thinking of horses, great horses, as she sat her horse.

Turning in a flash in the middle of the field she drove him on with her knees. They went at the wall together. Over the grasses, over the tufts and mounds, both knitted in excitement, the horse sprang to the surge of her heart as her eyes gazed between his ears at the blue top of the flint wall.

Enid Bagnold, *National Velvet*

25. *The Woman on the Roof***

The contours of the sprawling house, meaningless in silhouette, stood out against the washed-in backcloth of the lamplit street, and as his glance rested on one promontory, nearer to him and more curiously shaped than the rest, part of it moved.

He stood quite still, watching intently, his eyes growing slowly more accustomed to the light. The curve on the wall flattened and vanished and a moment later a figure appeared almost on a level with him and very much nearer than he had expected, so that he guessed there was some kind of platform—the roof of a bay window perhaps—directly below the window.

It was a woman on the roof. He caught a brief but clear glimpse of her as she passed through the shaft of light. His startled impression was of finery of some sort, a white hat with a mighty bow on it, and a bright scarf wrapped high round a small throat, Regency fashion. He did not see her face. She had been looking away from him down into the street. Her movements were furtive and she made very little sound, yet from sundry scrapings and shufflings he gathered that she was still there, very close to him just outside the window in the dark angle where the light did not reach.

By holding his breath he could just hear her moving and he wondered what on earth she was doing. If she was burgling she was certainly taking her time about it and Detective Officer Corkerdale's behaviour was astonishingly casual. Campion was venturing a half step closer when a piece of drapery passed once over the window. There was no repetition of this, but the rustling noises contened. Presently after a long pause the sash began to rise.

Margery Allingham, *More Work for the Undertaker*

26. *The Secret Sharer***

On my right there were lines of fishing stakes resembling a mysterious system of half-submerged bamboo fences, incomprehensible in its division of the domain of tropical fishes, and crazy of aspect as if abandoned for ever by some nomad tribe of fishermen now gone to the other end of the ocean; for there was no sign of human habitation as far as the eye could reach. To the left a group of barren islets, suggesting ruins of stone walls, towers, and blockhouses, had its foundations set in a blue sea that itself looked solid, so still and stable did it lie below my feet; even the track of light from the westering sun shone smoothly, without that animated glitter which tells of an imperceptible ripple. And when I turned my head to take a parting glance at the tug which had just left us anchored outside the bar, I saw the straight line of the flat shore joined to the stable sea, edge to edge, with a perfect and unmarked closeness, in one levelled floor half brown, half blue under the enormous dome of the sky. Corresponding in their insignificance to the islets of the sea, two small clumps of trees, one on each side of the only fault in the impeccable joint, marked the mouth of the river Meinam we had just left on the first preparatory stage of our homeward journey; and, far back on the inland level, a larger and loftier mass, the grove surrounding the great Paknam pagoda, was the only thing on which the eye could rest from the vain task of exploring the monotonous sweep of the horizon.

Joseph Conrad, 'Twixt Land and Sea Tales

27. The Oil Tanker*

She was an oil tanker they had grown rather fond of; she was the only tanker in a homeward-bound convoy of fifty ships which had run into trouble, and they had been cherishing her, as they sometimes cherished ships they recognized from former convoys, or ships with queer funnels, or ships that told lies about their capacity to keep up with the rest of the fleet. On this occasion, she had won their affection by being obviously the number one target of the attacking U-boats; on three successive nights they had sunk the ship ahead of her, the ship astern, and the corresponding ship in the next column; and as the shelter of land approached it became of supreme importance to see her through to the end of the voyage. But her luck did not hold; on their last day of the open sea, with the Scottish hills only just over the horizon, the attackers found their mark, and she was mortally struck.

She was torpedoed in broad daylight on a lovely sunny afternoon; there had been the usual scare, the usual waiting, the usual noise of an under-water explosion, and then, from this ship they had been trying to guard, a colossal pillar of smoke and flame came billowing out, and in a minute the long shapely hull was on fire almost from end to end.

Nicholas Monsarrat, The Cruel Sea

28. The Common Land***

The cabins stood on the brow of a hill. In winter they seemed to crouch beneath a sweeping wind—and the grass thatchings would have been whirled away if they had not been kept in position by ropes that were weighted with stones. The small irregular plots in which the villagers grew their potatoes were bounded by dry walls through crevices of which the wind whistled shrilly, and scattered with boulders too deeply imbedded to be worth the labour of moving, and the walls and boulders were alike covered with an ashen lichen that made them look as if they were crusted over with bitter salt that the wind had carried in from the sea. Between the garden plots lay a wilderness of common land, on which lean cattle grazed or routed among heaps of decaying garbage; in winter a desolation, in summer a purgatory of flies. But with the coming of evening and a softer air Clonderriff became transformed. One saw no longer the sordid details, only the long level lines of the bog, the whitewashed cabins shining milky as elder-blossom in moonlight, their windows bloomed with candlelight. In every cranny of the garden walls the crickets began their tingling chorus, but every other living thing in the village seemed at rest.

Francis Brett Young, The Tragic Bride

29. Country Life***

Cooking and washing-up were done in the back kitchen; the front kitchen was the family living and dining-room. In the fireplace a small sitting-room grate with hobs had replaced the fire on the hearth of a few years before; but the open chimney and chimney corners had been left, and from one of these a long, high-backed settle ran out into the room. In the space thus enclosed a red-and-black carpet had been laid to accommodate Miss Lane's chair at the head of the table and a few fireside chairs. This little room within a room was known as the hearthplace. Beyond it the stone floor was bare but for a few mats.

4—A.S.P.C.

Brass candlesticks and a brass pestle and mortar ornamented the high mantelshelf, and there were brass warming-pans on the walls, together with a few coloured prints; one, of the first man in this country to carry an umbrella—rain was coming down in sheets and he was followed by a jeering but highly ornamental crowd. A blue-and-white dish of oranges stuck with cloves stood upon the dresser. They were dry and withered at that time of the year, but still contributed their quota to the distinctive flavour of the air.

Everything was just as Miss Lane had inherited it. Except for a couple of easy chairs by the hearth, she had added nothing. 'What was good enough for my parents and grandparents is good enough for me', she would say when some of her more fashionable friends tried to persuade her to bring her house up to date. But family loyalty was rather an excuse than a reason for her preference; she kept the old things she had inherited because she enjoyed seeing and owning them.

Flora Thompson, *Lark Rise to Candleford*

30. *A Nice Place To Live****

And it was a nice place to live. The houses faced each other across the narrow cobbled street, steep and twisting like a gully in the rock because St Pierre was built upon the sheer precipitous face of the granite cliff and partook of the nature of the rock to which it held. But their propinquity did not detract from the dignity and beauty of the tall old houses. Their granite walls, built to stand as enduringly against the gales as the cliff itself, had been covered with pink stucco a century ago, and with the passing of the years the pink had weathered to every conceivable lovely shade of saffron, orange, yellow and old gold. Flights of shallow steps, scrubbed to a spotless white, flanked by fluted columns and beautiful iron railings and lantern holders, led up to handsome front doors with brass knockers beneath elegant fanlights, the windows were shuttered in the French style and the old tiled roofs had weathered to colours that equalled the stuccoed fronts in beauty. In front of the area railings, flanking the white steps and the fluted columns, grew the hydrangeas that were the glory of the island, pink and blue, grown to amazing luxuriance in the sheltered sunny warmth of the lovely street, and seen through opening front doors on summer days, through a vista of shining oak-panelled passage leading to garden doors set wide to the scent and colour, were the old deep gardens with their velvety lawns, their roses and jessamines and great magnolia trees, their myrtle and veronica bushes and lavender hedges, and tangled vines upon the sheltering granite walls.

Elizabeth Goudge, *Green Dolphin Country*

31. *The Procession****

'The procession is what matters most, tonight', he said, explaining how the circling of the church expressed the hesitation, the doubts of the Disciples, finding Christ vanished from the Sepulchre. Thus, the procession goes to search for Christ outside the walls, and the third time, accepts the miracle, entering again, to proclaim the Resurrection. Yea, verily He is Risen!

As we waited, the night air smelled damp and fresh, the scent of the early lilac in the courtyard overcoming the wafts of incense that floated from the church along with snatches of muffled chanting. At their windows the French householders stood silent, sharing something of the tension. Just before midnight the church doors swung open and in a flood of colour and candlelight the glittering procession emerged to circle the building three times, chanting.

The long tapers they carried sparkled on the sumptuous brocaded vestments and the diamond studded crowns of the Metropolitan and high clergy. Gold-coped priests and acolytes swung censers and carried the banners and ikons, all glowing out from the darkness. At last, with measured tread, grave in their joy, they re-entered the church, there to announce to the waiting throng that Christ was Risen. We heard a sudden burst of singing, rapturous music, and the bells rang out overhead.

Lesley Blanch, 'The Times Saturday Review'

32. *A Strange Convalescence****

While he was awaiting the convenience of the man who was to escort him back to England, Ronald deliberately ignored the scene around him. His fellow-patients, week by week, busied themselves with tennis, bed-making, toy-making, and their jazz orchestra. It was only much later that these scenes, which he had made an effort not to notice, returned to Ronald again and again accompanied by Dr. Fleischer's words—long after the specialist must have forgotten them—and mostly at the moments when Ronald, bored by his self-preoccupation, most wished to forget himself, clinics, hospitals, doctors, and all the pompous trappings of his malady. It was at these moments of rejection that the obsessive images of his early epileptic years bore down upon him and he felt himself to be, not the amiable johnnie he had by then, for the sake of sheer good will and protection from the world, affected to be—but as one possessed by a demon, judged by the probing inquisitors of life, an unsatisfactory clinic-rat which failed to respond to the right drug. In the course of time this experience sharpened his wits, and privately looking round at his world of acquaintances, he became, at certain tense moments, a truth-machine, under which his friends took on the aspect of demon-hypocrites. But being a reasonable man, he allowed these moods to pass over him, and in reality he rather liked his friends, and gave them his best advice when, in the following years, they began to ask him for it.

Muriel Spark, *The Bachelors*

Section 3. SOCIAL COMMENT

33. *Upward Mobility***

On the matter of how much upward mobility there really is in this country, thinking has fluctuated a great deal—more, perhaps, than the mobility itself. Forty years ago the notion that the U.S. had a fairly fluid society would not have been particularly controversial; observers did point out that the Alger story was more an article of faith than a reality, but for the most part they felt our social structure was dynamic —almost frighteningly so. During the thirties and forties, however, a highly influential series of community studies began convincing people that this was no longer so. Quite the contrary, it now appeared that the American system was finally shaking down into a fixed order of things in which achievement was more and more closed to the lower classes.

Anthropologist Lloyd Warner and others held that the basic pattern was revealed by the rigidities of the traditional community—the venerable, tree-shaded town in which the Hill, local business ties, and interlocking family relationships firmly fix the individual's position, and from which he can move upwards (from Elks, say, to Rotary) only by sanction of the next upper group. Shortcutting of this route, furthermore, was now believed to be more difficult than ever. The old route up through the shop was closing; the worker was unionized, the manager professionalized, and these lines firmed, the boy from the shanty-town was going to have less chance than ever of crossing over the tracks.

William H. Whyte, *The Organization Man*

34. *Controversial Issues****

Finally we come to the really controversial issues, those issues concerning which a considerable number of thoughtful people hold contrary opinions. Most very live current problems may be expected to fall under this head. Some of these are so important that pupils or students of the proper age and development should study them, partly to understand the different positions taken and reasons therefor, in order that each may form his own opinion, partly to learn, in the only way possible, how to deal intelligently with as yet unsolved social problems. In the degree that a problem is properly to be counted controversial will the true teacher refuse to let his own position prevent those under him from thinking fairly for themselves regarding it. The teacher must know that on such issues he is a public servant. He is not there to gain converts to his partisan cause; he is there to help those under his care learn to think reliably for themselves.

In the matter of controversial issues teachers must understand that, however or whatever they teach, they are none the less promoting one kind of society in preference to all others. If they refuse to teach controversial issues in any effective way, they are thereby educating either to uncritical acceptance or to uncritical rejection of new proposals; either of these is an education to inferior citizenship. That many people prefer youth to be so educated is only too true. The true teacher, however, cannot yield to such a reactionary attitude, he must educate those under his care to the best independent thinking he and they can effect. To this conclusion we seem inexorably led by our study of the philosophy of educative methods and democratic teaching.

William Heard Kilpatrick, *Philosophy of Education*

35. *Generalizing on Education***

Another consequence of the variety of institutions and the autonomy of local authorities is that it is almost impossible to describe anything acceptably in general terms. Claims for diversity can be overdone. Teachers and education officers often tend to overestimate the extent to which they are unique. Education in England and Wales is diverse, in the sense that experience of individual parents can be markedly different from one area to another and in different parts of the same area. It is homogeneous in that the pattern of provision (or lack of it), the various stages of education, the kind of things taught, the examinations taken, are all broadly similar. But the only generalization that one educationist will allow another is that you cannot make generalizations about English education. I believe the picture given in this book is substantially accurate. But there are bound to be people who can justly claim that what is said about a group of schools does not apply to their school, and there are bound to be organizations who can also claim that, whatever might be true of most bodies, it isn't true of them.

There is one further difficulty, which can be overcome only by an arbitrary decision on the part of the author. What should one call those schools which are part of the statutory system of education? 'Local authority schools' is too cumbersome and does not allow for the influence of national policy. 'County and voluntary schools' is what they are called in the Education Act, 1944, but that is too much of a mouthful too. Maintained schools is official but confusing. The obvious name should be 'public schools' because that is what they are, and the term neatly begs the question of who has the most control over them. But it has already been pre-empted by schools which are not in the least public, whatever else they may be.

Tyrrell Burgess, *A Guide to English Schools*

36. *Status of the Russian Teacher**

On the other hand, the social prestige of the teacher has risen. Politically, they are supported at all levels; socially, they play a part in local and national affairs out of all proportion to their numbers. The level of teachers' qualifications is improving, which is likely to increase their prestige. Education is also the most important road to advancement, which enhances the teacher's standing in the eyes of pupils and parents alike. Traditional regard for 'culture' helps too, the popular awe of the teacher as the fount of all wisdom was bound to vanish, but this does not mean that he can be dismissed as of no account. The present wage levels can hardly be called tempting, yet competition for entry to the pedagogic institutes is keen. Popular respect for education is high; the Soviet Union as a whole appears to value its teachers at least in the abstract. If the authorities were to back up their statements with cash, they would leave the teachers in no doubt at all of their importance to the community and the nation.

Nigel Grant, *Soviet Education*

37. *A Mythical Figure**

A. P. Herbert has drawn attention to the fact that the Common Law of England has been built around a mythical figure—the Reasonable Man— but that, although many legal cases are in the final analysis decided with reference to whether the actions involved were those of a reasonable man, no mention has ever been made in law of a reasonable woman. From this he draws the amusing conclusion that at Common Law the Reasonable Woman does not exist. At the same time, although legally noticed, the Reasonable Man who is reasonable in all things is as mythical as the Reasonable Woman. Every man is at times unreasonable even if only for the sake of enlivening an otherwise dull existence. Similarly there is no statistical or average man.

The average man does not exist. The average applies to a set of data and not to an individual and if the average man could exist he would be such an odd specimen that by his very uniqueness he would deny his own title. An assurance company, when fixing the premiums payable on its policies, is not concerned with its liability to one individual. Instead it is concerned about the total amount that it may be called upon to pay in benefits to the total number of policy holders. The average is, however, often misapplied to individuals.

W. J. Reichmann, *Use and Abuse of Statistics*

38. Correctional Treatment**

This involves treating a period of correctional treatment in prison as a specially designed form of experience intended to increase rather than reduce the prisoner's ability to get on outside after he leaves. As many existing contacts with the outside world as are likely to be helpful would therefore have to be maintained. Existing restrictions on visits and letters, for example, would have to go, in their present form. The incursion of the outside world would be limited only to the extent that it was felt to be harmful to the prisoner's progress. Thus the prison might become a protected social situation, in order that offenders, with their limited powers of adjustment, might be able to cope. Some limited isolation, carefully adjusted to the prisoner's own limitations, would then be justifiable. But as he became more competent, so more difficult tasks would be presented to him. More and more of the complicated problems of the outside world would be allowed to impinge upon him, until at last it was felt that he was ready for release.

In a prison like this, after-care would be merely a continuation, outside the institution, of the treatment which had begun within. From the very first day of a man's sentence, the efforts of the correctional staff would be directed towards increasing the area of his freedom, so that he might leave at the earliest possible moment. But it would not follow that when he was discharged he no longer needed help.

Howard Jones, *Crime in a Changing Society*

39. *Something Tasty****

'Something tasty' is the key-phrase in feeding; something solid, preferably meaty, and with a well defined flavour. The tastiness is increased by a liberal use of sauces and pickles, notably tomato sauce and piccalilli. I used to notice that in the flusher early years of married life my relatives were often frying at tea-times—chops, steak, kidney, chips. By contrast, poor old-age pensioners used sometimes to simulate a tasty meal by dissolving a penny Oxo in warm water, and having it with bread. Meat has been much relied upon since it first became really cheap, and any working-class wife who has known thin times will have a fine knowledge of those cuts which are inexpensive and nourishing and also tasty. The emphasis on tastiness shows itself most clearly in the need to provide 'something for tea', at weekends if not each day. There is a great range of favourite savouries, often by-products—black-puddings, pig's feet, liver, cowheel, tripe, polony, 'ducks', chitterlings (and for special occasions pork-pies, which are extremely popular); and the fishmonger's savouries—shrimps, roe, kippers and mussels. In our house we lived simply for most of the week; breakfast was usually bread and dripping, dinner a good simple stew; something tasty was provided for the workers at tea-time, but nothing costing more than a few coppers. At the weekend we lived largely; like everyone else except the very poor, and Sunday tea was the peak. By six on that evening the middens up the back had a fine topcoat of empty salmon and fruit tins.

Richard Hoggart, *The Uses of Literacy*

40. *The Summer Capital****

Walking about the streets of the summer capital once more, walking by spring sunlight, and a cloudless skirmishing blue sea—half-asleep and half-awake—I felt like the Adam of the mediaeval legends; the world-compounded body of a man whose flesh was soil, whose bones were stones, whose blood water, whose hair was grass, whose eyesight sunlight, whose breath was wind, and whose thoughts were clouds. And weightless now, as if after some long wasting illness, I found myself turned adrift again to float upon the shallows of Mareotis with its old tide-marks of appetites and desires refunded into the history of the place; an ancient city with all its cruelties intact, pitched upon a desert and a lake. Walking down with remembered grooves of streets which extended on every side, radiating out like the arms of a starfish from the axis of its founder's tomb. Footfalls echoing in the memory, forgotten scenes and conversations springing up at me from the walls, the cafe tables, the shuttered rooms with cracked and peeling ceilings. Alexandria, princess and whore. The royal city and the *anus mundi*. She would never change so long as the races continued to seethe here like must in a vat; so long as the streets and squares still gushed and spouted with the fermentation of these diverse passions and spites, rages and sudden calms. A fecund desert of human loves littered with the whitening bones of its exiles. Tall palms and minarets marrying the sky.

Lawrence Durrell, *Clea*

41. A Night in Wales*

The strangers, huddled against the wall, their hands deep in their pockets, their cigarettes sparkling, stared, I thought, at the thickening of the dark over the empty sands, but their eyes may have been closed. A train raced over us, and the arch shook. Over the shore, behind the vanishing train, smoke clouds flew together, rags of wings and hollow bodies of great birds black as tunnels, and broke up lazily; cinders fell through a sieve in the air, and the sparks were put out by the wet dark before they reached the sand. The night before, little quick scarecrows had bent and picked at the track-line and a solitary dignified scavenger wandered three miles by the edge with a crumpled coal sack and a park-keeper's steel-tipped stick. Now they were tucked up in sacks, asleep in a siding, their heads in bins, their beards in straw, in coal-trucks thinking of fires, or lying beyond pickings on Jack Stiff's slab near the pub in the Fishguard Alley, where the methylated-spirit drinkers danced into the policemen's arms and women like lumps of clothes in a pool waited, in doorways and holes in the soaking wall, for vampires or firemen.

Dylan Thomas, *Portrait of the Artist as a Young Dog*

42. Committees**

In a discussion on human happiness it was more or less generally agreed that to a certain type of character, both male and female but more often male, service on a committee is as real a compensation for daily ills as can be found. Life must always be a disappointing affair, full of tribulations and annoyances, misunderstandings and misrepresentations, worries domestic and financial, illnesses, mislaid letters and lost golf-balls, but for the few who are in a position to sit on committees it has consolation enough. No sooner do they enter the room, no sooner do they see the long table with its chairs not too close together and opposite each chair its blotting-paper and its writing-paper and its agenda paper, than they are translated into a new sphere of responsibility and service where content prevails. When one does public work the world of private mortifications fades away and one is permeated by a sense of importance. No man or woman permeated by a sense of importance can be miserable for long.

But if the rank and file are thus exalted and soothed, what of the chairmen? If there are happier men than chairmen of committees I should like to see them. A newly-elected M.P. may be more pompous. The captain of a ship and a schoolmaster may equally have more power. Any kind of athletic champion may be prouder. But there is trouble ahead for all of these. The M.P. must some day reach St Stephen's, where he will become a nonentity; the captain will be anxious in fog and storm; the schoolmaster has to deal with parents; the champion's serenity will be undermined by the certainty that he is soon to be superseded. But the chairman of the committee's triumph is so gentle and unchallenged, and his sway is absolute.

E. V. Lucas, *Selected Modern English Essays*

Section 4. SCIENCE

43. *The Unbounded Universe***

The property of gravitational masses to deflect light rays explains why our universe is unbounded. For, although light rays travel in straight lines in the vast regions of space between the stars, they will be deflected when passing near the stars. And, if light rays suffer enough successive deflections, they can be caused to turn completely around and face in the opposite direction, in the same way the traveller does when he is half way round the earth. And, like the earth voyager who returns to his starting point by continually travelling in a straight line on the earth's surface, a space traveller in our universe would also find himself back at the earth if he travels what appears to him to be a straight line in space. He would no more know that he is travelling a gigantic circle in space than the earth voyager is conscious of travelling in a circle on the earth. In general, a straight line in space, then, is the path a light beam takes, which may be straight, or curved, or a combination of both. In order to avoid confusion with what we ordinarily think of as a straight line, we will refer to the lines in which light travels as space lines rather than straight lines in space.

James A. Coleman, *Relativity For The Layman*

44. *The Age and Evolution of the Stars****

We can endeavour to obtain guidance from theoretical considerations. If, for instance, a certain amount of matter is aggregated together to form a star, can we predict what its size and candle power will be? We are at once face to face with the difficulty that we know nothing about the composition of the interior of a star. Observation tells us a great deal about the composition of the outer layer, which is the only portion we can actually see. But can we necessarily assume that the composition of the matter deep in the interior of the stars is in any way similar to the composition of the outermost layer? Furthermore, we have no direct knowledge of the state of the matter in the interior. Are we justified in assuming that a star is gaseous throughout? The pressure at a great depth in the star is enormous; it is possible that the central portions of the stars may be liquefied by the high pressure to which they are subjected. All that we can do is to make assumptions, which may or may not represent an approximation to the actual conditions; then to work out the consequence of these assumptions and see whether they are in agreement or in conflict with the results of observations.

Suppose we make the assumption that the star is gaseous throughout and that the material everywhere has the properties which we can study in the laboratory, of what is termed a 'perfect gas'. It is evident that the density, pressure and temperature will all increase continually from the surface of the star inwards to the centre. Calculation shows that, under these assumptions, the temperature within a star of the same size and of the same weight as the Sun must exceed one million degrees throughout the greater part of the interior and that at the centre it must be many millions of degrees.

Spencer Jones, *Worlds Without End*

45. *Philosophical Background of Alchemy***

The use of cover names was, however, the least part of the symbolism employed. The Great Work of alchemy was intimately bound up with the whole religious and philosophical background, and for many who practised it the transmutation of metals was symbolical of the transmutation of imperfect man into a state of perfection. Conversely, metallic transmutation could be brought about only by divine aid and by men of pure life. These two tenets reacted upon one another and are complexly interwoven in alchemical thought. The unity of the world and all things in it was an unshakable belief; there was thus nothing illogical in the combination of mystical theology with practical chemistry, however incongruous it may seem to us today. It is this combination that accounts for the extraordinary character of the bulk of serious alchemical literature; serious as opposed to the clearly fraudulent writings of the charlatans and to those of men who derided what was in fact a philosophy of life. It is also this combination that often makes it very difficult to decide whether a particular work of symbolism is intended to convey real chemical information, or whether it is to be taken as speculative thought.

E. J. Holmyard, *Alchemy*

46. Sewing Threads**

For all garment seams the sewing thread should possess high strength, high resistance to degradation, and good stability to all expected making-up, laundering and cleaning conditions.

Mercerized cotton threads provide satisfactory initial strength in most seams but degrade in wear, for example in armhole seams due to perspiration. Synthetic fibre sewing threads have the advantage of increased strength and much superior resistance to degradation in wear. Their extra strength can be utilized either to produce a stronger seam with the same size of sewing threads, or to obtain the same strength of seam using a much finer thread, with the resultant production of a neater seam.

Seam puckering is probably the most obvious fault in the appearance of garments, and an important factor in its elimination is the choice of a suitable sewing thread. Puckering may be caused by contraction of seams owing to shrinkage of threads either in laundering or due to recovery from extension. A first essential is therefore that the thread be stable to all expected laundering conditions. Secondly, since even the most carefully adjusted machine exerts some tension, causing extension of the sewing thread when forming a stitch, highly elastic threads which stretch easily may cause puckering by contraction immediately after the stitch is formed. Ideally a sewing thread should be made from a fibre with a high initial modulus constructed into a yarn which allows a small permanent yield under tension.

I.C.I., *Making-up Processes*

47. Computers**

After one has learned something about the extremely rapid development of computers since World War Two, one inevitably wonders whether there are any foreseeable limits to their future development. In this connection, it is interesting to make a few approximate comparisons between computer characteristics and some of the characteristics of the human brain. The basic cell of the human nervous system is known as a neuron. When neurons are suitably stimulated they absorb or emit nerve impulses, which travel along fibres called axons. A neuron is about the size of a large organic molecule—that is, about a hundred-thousandth of a centimetre in diameter—while the axons sometimes extend for several feet. The disturbance generated by the neuron travels along the axon as an electrical pulse; concurrent with this electrical activity along the axon there also occur chemical changes. The nerve impulses travel the axon at various speeds, but the highest is thought to be in the neighbourhood of ten thousand centimetres a second. This should be compared with the speed of light, which is also the speed at which electrical signals travel in a computer—about thirty billion centimetres a second. (According to Einstein's theory of relativity, the speed of light is also the maximum speed at which any signal can travel.) The human brain, which weighs about a pound, has a volume of about a thousand cubic centimetres and contains about ten billion neurons.

J. Bernstein, *The Analytical Engine*

48. Camouflage**

Whilst the camouflage of cryptic coloration provides us with such clear examples of a creative element in natural selection, the more specialized phenomena of mimicry show us refinements in the process which would indeed seem incredible were it not for the fact that we see many steps which, whilst not on the direct road to the finest examples, give us every confidence in the theory we believe to underlie the method of their creation. The term 'mimicry', I should explain for those who are not biologists, has for us a special limited meaning. In some books on popular natural history the term may be loosely used in regard to some of the adaptations I have just been speaking of, as when it may be said that a particular insect mimics a leaf or a stick; that is true in plain English, but it has by convention been reserved by biologists for a particular type of coloration. It implies that one animal is mimicking another animal, but we must think of the word 'mimicking' in quotes, because what we really mean is that the evolutionary process has produced in one animal an imitation of another without any conscious act of mimicking. Now to explain mimicry I must discuss for a moment that other type of adaptive coloration given the name of 'warning' . . .

Sir Alister Hardy, *The Living Stream*

49. *Linguistic Thought****

Linguistic thought was developed to enable man to deal with the material world; but it would appear that such verbal expression does not usually take a part in dream structure. Need we assume, however, that if survival occurs at all it must necessarily be of a verbally reasoning kind? It would be fantastic, but perhaps just possible, I suppose, to conceive, if the evidence for survival should be overwhelming, that some non-linguistic dream-like personality might be able to manifest itself to us verbally, with difficulty, in some extra-sensory fashion through the speech centres of a medium, or those controlling writing. It is well to recall that the mystics can rarely express the rapture of their experience in linguistic terms and artists find it easier to depict their joy in colour, shape or sound than describe it in words. Creative writing, I believe, is much harder work than painting; an author is using his cortex to express and reason out what he feels on another level. Perhaps Shakespeare was right and, in our fundamental nature, we really are 'such stuff as dreams are made of'. Perhaps in depths we do belong to a world of Polany's 'tacit' knowledge and feeling to which the reasoning mind by itself is almost blind; a world which little children find it easier to imagine and to enter than do their verbally encrusted and over-pedantic elders. Such an apparently absurd idea is almost certainly far from the truth, but to have some imaginative picture in mind, however wrong, helps to combat the perhaps too pessimistic concept of sheer impossibility which would prejudice our judgement from the start. We must have an open mind.

Sir Alister Hardy, The Divine Flame

50. *Complexities of the Human Organism***

Some of the complexities characterizing the human organism can be seen in simple organisms, with their membranes acting as selectors with respect to stimuli in the surrounding environment. The protoplasm itself has certain basic qualities of irritability, excitability and transmissibility which take the form of gradients of activation that spread like waves across a pond. This is the complete picture in the simplest sorts of organism, resulting in the simplest of behavioural responses. This can also be seen in the simple reflex actions in man, such as jumping at a sudden loud sound, or blinking at a flash of light. An amoeba, for example, the simplest of organisms, being just one proto-plasmic cell, shows all the characteristics of 'life' and will respond to a pin-prick by retreating from the point of stimulation.

When we compare many different organisms, it is apparent that the organization and patterns demonstrated, are very similar for a great variety of different forms. Symmetry and polarity are examples of such characteristic general features. However, as we start proceeding up the evolutionary scale to more and more complex organisms—from the earthworm to the great apes—these characteristics become complicated by the process of differentiation. Large groups of cells become organized systems which perform special functions contributing towards the well-being of the organism-as-a-whole.

F. H. George, *Automation Cybernetics and Society*

51. *Biological Organization***

This agreement is not, as one might think, a sheer coincidence; on the contrary. If the activities of an object are to be intelligible at all, its material structure must be of such a kind as to make these activities possible. Unless the solar system had the sort of structure it does, eclipses could not occur; though the layout is one thing and the eclipses are another, it is by studying the disposition of the different bodies in the system that we understand how eclipses are possible, and on what conditions they take place. In the same way, when we have fully sur-veyed the 'layout' of the DNA molecule, we shall presumably come to see how replication, too, is possible, and on what conditions it will take place—why a molecule of that design, placed in the right conditions, could not fail to replicate. Expanding and refining the concept of organization, one must expect similar correlations at other levels. Biological organization is not the same as life; but it is, clearly enough, the material prerequisite for life. Only in a creature with the necessary organization are vital and mental activities possible and intelligible; and we must understand this organization if we are ever to explain the possibility of life, and the conditions needed for its occurrence.

Stephen Toulmin and June Goodfield, *The Architecture of Matter*

Section 5. PHILOSOPHICAL and PSYCHOLOGICAL

52. *Becoming Individual****

It is quite clear that here neither the idea of the community nor the idea of the individual reach their fulfilment, but that here they stand in a historically and psychologically necessary, but nevertheless penultimate stage of their development. The Leader serves his office. But this service of his office is itself only penultimate. The individual experiences in the authority of an office his commitments, his restrictions, but at the same time his responsibility. Even here, however, man is not yet seen as he is. Only when man sees that office is a penultimate authority in the face of an ultimate, indescribable authority, in the face of the authority of God, has the real situation been reached. And before this authority the individual knows himself to be completely alone. The individual is responsible before God. And this solitude of man's position before God, this subjection to an ultimate authority, is destroyed when the authority of the Leader of office is seen as ultimate authority. The irrefutable sign of man's individuality is that he must die alone, that he must bear his body for himself, that he must bear his suffering and his guilt as an individual. Alone before God, man becomes what he is, free and committed in responsibility at the same time. He becomes an individual.

Dietrich Bonhoeffer, No Rusty Swords

53. *A Blind Alley***

Is life an open road or a blind alley? This question, barely formulated a few centuries ago, is today explicitly on the lips of mankind as a whole. As a result of the brief, violent moment of crisis in which it became conscious at once of its creative power and of its critical faculties, humanity has quite legitimately become hard to move; no stimulus at the level of mere instinct or blind economic necessity will suffice for long to goad it into moving onwards. Only a reason, and a valid and important reason, for loving life passionately will cause it to advance further. But where, at the experimental level, are we to find, if not a complete justification, at least the beginnings of a justification of life? Only, it would seem, in the consideration of the intrinsic value of the phenomenon of man. Continue to regard man as an accidental outgrowth or sport of nature and you will drive him into a state of disgust or revolt which, if it became general, would mean the definitive stoppage of life on earth. Recognize, on the other hand, that within the domain of our experience man is at the head of one of the two greatest waves into which, for us, tangible reality is divided, and that therefore he holds in his hands the fortunes of the universe; and immediately you cause him to turn his face towards the grandeur of a new sunrise.

Teilhard de Chardin, *Hymn of the Universe*

54. Lust and Love*

This is, of course, not easy. It is much easier to lust than to love; much easier to make demands and to call it love than to give love. To love is always to be vulnerable to hurt. Love costs and may be rejected. Because of our insecurity, of our lack of self awareness, we fear to love and prefer to lust—to demand affection. This demand will also and even more certainly bring rejection, because the demands become intolerable and kill what love was there. But there is a difference between the loneliness which follows the rejection of the true self-giving love and the loneliness that follows the demanding love; the former learns the value and meaning of love, the latter learns only bitterness and self pity. Christ on the Cross was rejected, and through that rejection men found the life of love which casts out fear. There is much to learn of love in the prayer of St. Francis; 'let me not seek to be consoled so much as to console, to be understood as much as to understand, to be loved as much as to love. For it is in giving that we receive, it is in forgetting ourselves that we find ourselves, it is in forgiving that we are forgiven, and it is in dying that we are raised up into eternal life.'

Douglas Rhymes, *No New Morality*

55. *The Doctrine of the Tao****

Tao is the original, the uncarved block, the unity behind all multi-
plicity, for if the block is carved there will be distinctions and names,
and opposition to the unity of nature. Or Tao is like a drifting boat
going where it wills, covering creatures yet not mastering them, lowly,
yet great through that. So the quietist acts without action, and does
without doing; for those who speak do not know, but those who know
do not speak. So since the way of Heaven is to sharpen without cutting,
the way of the sage is to act without striving.

It would be easy to parody this doctrine as mere laziness and ineffec-
tiveness, but the whole burden of the teaching is the power that comes
from complete harmony with nature, and the self-defeat of fussy
activity. It seems that in the fourth and third centuries B.C. the
Chinese had begun to learn of people and customs outside their own
vast land, and so the more thoughtful sought inner peace in face of the
increasing distractions of the outer world. They looked back to the
remote past, when it was assumed that an ideal state existed, more
simple and natural, when sage ancestors ruled vast empires by action-
less activity. But this is a model to the present, and amid the quarrels of
China's states the Tao Te Ching, more than other books of the same
school roundly condemns warfare; though self-protection may be
justified, yet offensive war is against the whole interest of mankind, and
this is addressed to rulers and wordly people as well as to quietists.

Geoffrey Parrinder, *The World's Living Religions*

56. *Suicide of a Nation?***

One of the most striking features of British industry is that its people
are virtually devoid of ambition, at least by the standards plainly in
evidence in the United States. Labourers fight shy of becoming foremen.
Foremen rarely dream of managing a plant of their own and are as
rarely asked to do so. And if managers graduate to tycoons they are
likely to be singled out in the columns of the Financial Times as exceptional men.

Resignation also makes management effete, for there is nothing else
to explain why industries of all sizes seem to prefer to maintain prices
in a stable and comfortable market than to vary them in quest of more

business and bigger profits. Its unwillingness to do anything for the first time is another symptom of underlying passivity. Thus the acknowledged niggardliness of British Industry towards research is much more a consequence of moral depression than of shortage of capital. There is no reason, after all, why the machine tool industry, and the ship building industry, should not have designed a decade ago the programmes of innovation the Department of Scientific and Industrial Research would now wish upon them.

In short, Britain has to come to grips with its place in the world. A people which chronically expects too little at home consistently expects too much abroad.

Arnold Lunn and Garth Lean, *The New Morality*

57. *A Natural Symbol****

It is normal for a man to resist his anima because she represents, as I said before, the unconscious with all those tendencies and contents hitherto excluded from conscious life. They were excluded for a number of real and apparent reasons. Some are suppressed and some are repressed. As a rule those tendencies that represent the amount of anti-social elements in man's psychical structure—what I call the 'statistical criminal' in everybody—are suppressed, that is, consciously and deliberately disposed of. But tendencies that are merely repressed are usually only doubtful in character. They are not indubitably anti-social, but are rather unconventional and socially awkward. The reason why one represses them is equally doubtful. Some people repress them from sheer cowardice, others from a merely conventional morality, and others again from the motive of respectability. Repression is a sort of half-conscious and half-hearted letting go of things, a dropping of hot cakes or a reviling of grapes which hang too high, or a looking the other way in order not to become conscious of one's desires. Freud has discovered repression as one of the main mechanisms in the making of a neurosis. Suppression amounts to a conscious moral choice, but repression is a rather immoral 'penchant' for getting rid of disagreeable decisions.

C. G. Jung, *Psychology and Religion*

58. By Dint of Multitudes**

Life advances by mass effects, by dint of multitudes flung into action without apparent plan. Milliards of germs and millions of adults jostling, shoving, and devouring one another, fight for elbow room and for the best and largest living space. Despite all the waste and ferocity, all the mystery and scandal it involves, there is, as we must be fair and admit, a great deal of biological efficiency in the *struggle for life*. In the course of this implacable contest between masses of substance in irresistible expansion, the individual unit is undeniably tried to the limit of its strength and resources. 'Survival of the fittest by natural selection' is not a meaningless expression, provided it is not taken to imply either a final ideal or a final explanation.

But it is not the individual unit that seems to count for most in the phenomenon. What we find within the struggle for life is something deeper than a series of duels; it is a conflict of chances. By reckless self-reproduction life takes its precautions against mishap. It increases its chances of survival and at the same time multiplies its chances of progress.

Teilhard de Chardin, The Phenomenon of Man

59. God's Own Act of Self-negation**

In the light of the Hegelian vision, Altizer interprets the 'death of God' as God's own act of self-negation or self-annihilation. God ceases to have any reality as the primordial Being, impassive, unmoving, eternal, wholly isolated from the processes of time and history. In Jesus Christ he has emptied himself into the transiency and flux of flesh with all its ambiguity and impurity. Now he has his being solely in the forward movement of process. Altizer contends that God remains God even in sacrificing himself wholly to the creaturely reality. But his presence in process amounts to a kind of self-estrangement within his own being, for in the Incarnation God alienates himself from the transcendence and abstractness of his pre-incarnate form. Since the actualization of the former requires the negation of the latter, Altizer insists on the legitimacy of speaking of the 'death of God'. God is dead, irrecoverably surpassed, as the empty and alien 'Other' who in heavenly isolation remains untouched and unaffected by the world process. His movement into process has resulted in a radical transformation of his own Being.

Transcendence has been transmuted wholly into immanence. This is the meaning of the Christian affirmation of the 'death of God'.

Thomas W. Ogletree, *The 'Death of God' Controversy*

60. *Philosophy and Science***

But there are two different ways in which a philosophy may seek to base itself upon science. It may emphasize the most general results of science, and seek to give even greater generality and unity to these results. Or it may study the methods of science, and seek to apply these methods, with the necessary adaptations, to its own peculiar province. Much philosophy inspired by science has gone astray through pre-occupation with the results momentarily supposed to have been achieved. It is not results, but methods, that can be transferred with profit from the sphere of the special sciences to the sphere of philosophy. What I wish to bring to your notice is the possibility and importance of applying to philosophical problems certain broad principles of method which have been found successful in the study of scientific questions.

The opposition between a philosophy guided by scientific method and a philosophy dominated by religious and ethical ideas may be illustrated by two notions which are very prevalent in the works of philosophers, namely the notion of the universe, and the notion of good and evil. A philosopher is expected to tell us something about the nature of the universe as a whole, and to give grounds for either optimism or pessimism.

Bertrand Russell, *Mysticism and Logic*

61. *A Comforting Argument****

Further, to think of human life in terms of its lowest factors, considered as in themselves dignified, has a curious effect in dignifying the individual concerned; makes him a type, and so something larger and more significant than before; makes his dignity feel safer, since he is sure he has at least these qualifications for it; makes him feel accepted and approved of by his herd, in that he is being humble and understanding their situation (poor creatures); makes it seem likely, since he understands their situation, because he feels it in himself, that they will return to him also this reserved and detached sympathy; makes him, indeed, feel grander than the rest of his herd, for a new series of reasons; because by thinking of them he has got outside them; because by forming a concept of them he has made them seem limited; because he has thereby come to seem less subject to the melancholy truths he is recognizing; because to recognize melancholy truths is itself, if you can be protected somehow, an invigorating activity; and (so that we complete the circle back to humility) because to think about these common factors has a certain solidity and safety in that it is itself, after all, one of the relevant common factors of the human mind.

William Empson, *Seven Types of Ambiguity*

Section 6. THE ARTS

62. *True Knowledge***

Again, in the same connection, he writes: 'It was natural that in the earliest times the inventor of any art which goes beyond the common-sense perceptions of mankind should be universally admired, not merely for any utility to be found in his inventions, but for the wisdom by which he was distinguished from other men. But when a variety of arts had been invented, some of them being concerned with the necessities and others with the social refinements of life, the inventors of the latter were naturally always considered wiser than the former because their knowledge was not directed to immediate utility. Hence when everything of these kinds had been already provided, those sciences were discovered which deal neither with necessities nor with the enjoyments of life, and this took place earliest in regions where men had leisure. This is why the mathematical arts were first put together in Egypt, for in that country the priestly caste were indulged with leisure.' Again the main point deserves emphasis. We owe the beginning of a true knowledge of reality to the leisured priests of Egypt, not to the technicians who found out how to do things.

Benjamin Farrington, Greek Science

63. *The Glitter of Kitchen Ware****

There was no room for such a procedure in Velazquez' artistic purpose. The problems which interest him throughout his life are very different from those that interest Raphael or Rubens. There is no question for him of filling spaces with figures whose grouping, lines and colours shall produce a determined effect of composition or decoration—his is an attempt to grasp the poetry of the living world. Naturalist painting in Velazquez reaches its extreme limit. It is not a question of imitation in the depreciatory sense of the term used by modern critics. Things lie before us in all their many-coloured, enchanting variety. A moment comes when an artist feels the lyric appeal of that diversity; from this springs the painting of qualities, those humble qualities of things disdained by Renaissance and Mannerist painters. Silks have one sheen and velvets another; a horse's glossy flanks are a delight to the sensitive eye, so too the silver embroidery on a black dress or the gleam of Milanese armour. Coming down to more humble things, the glitter of kitchen ware, the sparkle of wine in a brimming jug, fruits and dishes, have as rich pictorial qualities as gold chains or lace handkerchieves in ladies' hands. For the sensitive painter, delighting in the spectacle of the world, what a pleasing mission that of re-creating on his canvas the variety of the things that meet our eyes—revealing to us, so to say, the rich imagination of God himself.

Enrique Lafuente, *Velazquez*

64. *Goya as a Portraitist****

Goya's gifts as a portraitist are triumphantly displayed on this occasion. The famous portrait of the actress Doña Antonia Zárate in the Beit collection has extraordinary magic; it is a symphony in yellow and black. The exhibition may well help to break down one of the clichés so often employed about Goya—that he was a satirical portrait painter. The impression made here is rather of a portraitist who used his sitters as an excuse for combinations of colour; assessment of personality, although there, was not the dominating impulse in his make-up. There is little evidence to suggest that he was scoring off his clients even when he came to paint Ferdinand and his court; he used a 'realist' manner current in the late eighteenth century. If anything, the character of his portraits would suggest that he was on good terms with his sitters (though some doubtless bored him) and that, in the period before the war wracked the country, he was an enchanting poet of rank and fashion.

No hint of the caricature, no shade of indifference disturbs his exquisite portrait of La Condesa de Chinchón, who was the daughter of the Infante Don Luis and the wife of the all-powerful statesman, Godoy. In a note on the picture in the catalogue reference is made to its classical simplicity; and one is aware that Goya had studied not only the classics of Mengs but above all Velazquez. He is alert to the charms of a great lady but also to the task of placing her figure in space, off-setting the neutral colour of the background by the sheen of her dress, as delicately painted as in a Terborch.

Denys Sutton, 'Goya: Apostle of Reason'

65. *A Sure Measure****

Metalwork, from the beginning, has been a sure and precise measure of Spanish culture and of Spanish greatness; and there is nothing strange in this, for Spain has always been pre-eminently a mineral land. The first germs of civilization were implanted by the Phoenician and Greek colonists, who came exclusively to trade in metals, principally silver, gold, lead, and iron; and references to the mining of these metals may be found in the classical writers.

In caves and the rudimentary dwelling houses of the age in which these first elements of civilization made their appearance, one finds dross and other indications of the mining of the precious metals, chiefly of silver. There is, however, the noteworthy fact that no object made of such metals has been found among the household furniture of these dwelling places; nor are there any scraps of the metals themselves. This indicates that during the neolithic period the metals were worked by foreigners alone, and that they worked them solely for export; the natives not having realized their commercial value.

In spite of this, it was actually in the Cave of the Bats, belonging to the neolithic period, that the first Spanish ornament in precious metal was discovered; a smooth gold crown, undoubtedly made from pure metal, which appears to have been worked into a sheet of practically uniform thickness, by being hammered upon a stone, and then trimmed with a stone hatchet, producing a section thicker in the centre than at the edge.

Later, both the conditions of mining and the customs of the native changed; plates of silver, or iron, or sometimes copper or bronze, are found among their household goods. This shows that, in this second period, the people had either learnt the use of metals and worked them for themselves, or that foreign metalworkers, for the most part Phoenicians, had settled in Spain.

P. M. de Artiñano, Metalwork

66. *The Burial****

This is a representation of the miracle which is supposed to have happened when the Knight Orgaz was being buried in the church of San Tomé; Saints Augustine and Stephen were said to have appeared and relieved the priests of their work. In the colours of a storm sky, in

grey and yellow, white and black, Greco painted this miracle. The yellow
in the garments of both saints has the same unearthly light as the yellow
of the cloud edges in the arch; the black in the clothes of the chain of
spectators gives the foreground the same relief-depth as the abrupt
black beside the hard whites in the upper regions. Like the contour of
a rapidly rising and falling wave is the outline of the four illuminated
figures in the foreground; steeply upwards and downwards about the
grey monk on the left, in mutually inclined curves about the yellow of
the two saints, and again steeply upwards and downwards about the
soft figure, his back towards the spectator, of the priest on the right.
The depth of the wave indicates the optical centre, the double curve of
the saint's yellow garments is carried by the greyish white of the shroud
down still farther; in this lowest depth rests the bluish-grey armour of
the knight. This line-movement in the lower plane corresponds with
a line moving in the opposite sense in the upper vault, but even stronger
than the movements of the outlines is the colour-movement of yellow
and black above and beneath. This purely technical restlessness has a
counterpoise in the rigid repose of the content. Like pale pillars of salt,
all the figures and torch-flames and cloud-shapes seem to congeal in one
everlasting moment, and even the five astonished hands are motionless
as the gestures of harshly illuminated sculpture.

L. Goldscheider, *El Greco*

67. *The Modern Movement****

The modern movement in art has so often been presented as in itself
corrupt that it may seem paradoxical to represent it as a purifying
experience. But such it is and has been from the moment that Cézanne
resolved to 'realize his sensations in the presence of nature'. In retrospect the whole of this movement, in spite of its deviations and irregu-
larities, must be conceived as an immense effort to rid the mind of that
corruption which, whether it has taken the form of fantasy building or
repression, sentimentality or dogmatism, constitutes a false witness to
sensation or experience. Our artists have often been violent or destruc-
tive, inconsiderate or impatient, but in general they have been aware of
a moral issue, which is the moral issue facing the whole of our civilization.
Philosophy and politics, science and government, all rest finally on the
clarity with which we perceive and conceive the facts of experience, and
art has always been, directly through its artists and poets and indirectly

through the use which other people make of the signs and images invented by these artists and poets, the primary means of forming clear ideas of feelings and sensations. Individual artists may have introduced confusion into the general aim, but in the minds of the great leaders of the modern movement in painting—Cézanne, Matisse, Picasso, Kandinsky, Klee, Mondrian, and Pollock—there was always a constant awareness of the problem of our age, always a constant alertness to false solutions.

Herbert Read, *A Concise History of Modern Painting*

68. *A Barbarian of Genius****

Here again he is nobody's pupil, and we have no alternative but to put him down in the history of painting as an exceptional artist, a barbarian of genius who bawls out coloured prayers in an original dialect, an outlandish tongue.

His tempestuous soul goes from one extreme to another, restless and storm-tossed even during moments of deliberate repose; but just as it is deeply moving when meditating on the episodes of the Passion, so it is erratic and well-nigh baroque when reflecting on the joys of the Nativity. The truth is that it simpers and stammers when there is no torturing to be done, for Grünewald is the painter of tombs rather than cribs, and he can only depict the Virgin successfully when he makes her suffer. Otherwise he sees her as red-faced and vulgar, and there is such a difference between his Madonnas of the sorrowful mysteries and his Madonnas of the joyful mysteries that one wonders whether he was not following an aesthetic system, a scheme of intentional antitheses.

It is, indeed, quite likely that he decided that the quality of divine Motherhood would only come out clearly under the stress of the suffering endured at the foot of the cross. This theory would certainly fit in with the one he adopted whenever he wished to glorify the divine nature of the Son, for he always painted the living Christ as the Psalmist and Isaiah picture him—as the poorest and ugliest of men—and only restored his divine appearance to him after his Passion and death. In other words, Grünewald made the ugliness of the crucified Messiah the symbol of all the sins of the world which Christ took upon himself, thus illustrating a doctrine which was expounded by Tertullian, St. Cyprian, St. Cyril, St. Justin and countless others, and which was current for a good part of the Middle Ages.

Joris-Karl Huysmans, *Paintings of Grünewald*

69. *Artistic Tradition***

There seems to have been a weight of public opinion, almost certainly shared by all successful artists, in favour of the view that there was only one artistic tradition worth following. It may well be that this reflects the comfortable life of the citizens of these well organized empires. It may equally be a function of filial respect. The Romans reverenced the traditions of the ancestors and strove to keep their portraits in the home, as a living tradition in the hearts of the family. The Chinese respected the ancestors and remembered them with little offerings before the tablets with their names. Once a tradition has been established, this attitude of respect for the past tended to confirm it, in its essentials, for the duration of the whole civilization.

In such a world the formal art has moved far indeed from the traditionalism of the savage; and it may well have been divorced from the life of the ordinary people. Nevertheless it was probably not so, because, in the study of popular folk-arts within our own civilization, we find time and again that the people preserve aspects of the conventional aristocratic arts of earlier times. The art of a culture seems to belong to all the people. Every man has the possibility of producing art quite as simply as if he were still a savage. But, in the metropolitan civilizations, he has only the possibility of becoming a famous specialist in the arts if he puts most of his effort into learning his trade as an artist . . . and if he conforms to popular ideas of art.

C. A. Burland, Man and Art

70. *Spanish Art**

Spain is a world apart from the rest of Europe, separated by climatic differences and isolated in time as well as in space. Bounded by water on three sides, and on the fourth cut off by the barrier of the Pyrenees, she was for three hundred years, from the VIIIth to the XIth centuries, virtually under the domination of an oriental power—that of the Moors, whose culture was not only more advanced than that of any part of Europe, but also profoundly different from any European civilization. Their last stronghold in the Peninsula, Granada, only fell to the Christians at the end of the XVth century.

During the period of Moorish domination Islamic and Christian culture vied with one another for predominance and their interaction was considerable; but whereas Christian influence on the Moors was merely transitory, lasting only as long as they remained in the Peninsula, Moorish influence on the character and culture of the Spanish people was permanent. Artistically, Moorish influence lasted longest in architecture and the industrial arts; in painting it was short lived and confined to illustrated manuscripts. The history of Spanish painting proper can therefore be said to date from the beginning of the Christian reconquest of the Peninsula, when, through the consolidation of Christianity, Spain was brought into contact with Western European influences.

Enriqueta Harris, *Spanish Painting*

71. '*Automatism*'*

A comparable theorist of the opposing school of abstraction has not yet arisen, though one may find psychological justifications of it, and the surrealist theories of 'automatism' were perhaps an inspiration to the movement. But here the distinction that has to be made is between the spontaneous projection of unconscious (more properly speaking, pre-conscious) imagery, and the recognition, in chance effects or spontaneous gestures, of forms that have an uncalculated and indeterminate significance. A graphologist will find a person's handwriting significant, and will generally prefer to look at it upside down in order not to be distracted from a contemplation of its form as distinct from its literal meaning. Abstract Expressionism, as a movement in art, is but an extension and elaboration of this calligraphic expressionism, and that is why it has a close relationship to the Oriental art of calligraphy.

Herbert Read, *A Concise History of Modern Painting*

72. *Gilding and Painting***

The physical protection of gilding and painting dates back to the Christian gold-glass of the third and fourth centuries, but this seldom reaches private hands; abroad there is a production for tourists. The technique was revived in the first quarter of the eighteenth century by the Bohemians. It was precision work, two walls being used for each vessel, one fitting exactly into the other. The inner wall projected a quarter of an inch or so above the outer, and this projection was thicker than the rest and cut with a flange so that it could rest upon the outer wall. Before insertion it was ornamented with gold leaf and etched with a needle; silver leaf and colour could be incorporated. The joint between the rim of the outer wall and the flange of the inner had to be an exact one; it was cemented by some colourless adhesive and masked by a further decorative band of 'inserted gold'. Finally the complete vessel was submitted to the wheel and cut with fairly narrow vertical flutes from base to rim; hence the term 'many sided' which is frequently but erroneously applied to the little beakers and graceful goblets made in this fashion. The base of the beaker had a circular disc cut away from the outer skin; another disc was given a simple ruby and gold 'insertion' and cemented into place.

The designs chosen corresponded to those on surface-engraved glasses; hunting scenes were extremely popular, armorials frequent, and devotional subjects varied. Designs emblematic of the Four Seasons occur, and also of the Continents, again Four, since Australia had still to be discovered.

E. Barrington Haynes, Glass through the Ages

73. Drama**

Drama, then, had its strength in the faithful attendance of a middle-class audience, both in London and the provinces; it relied on the attractions of the conventional form of theatre; and sharpened its appeal with the new authority of the producer. In the main there was nothing particularly adventurous to set against the growing attractions of the cinema. The theatre was certainly ill-prepared to meet the next new medium of entertainment, television.

At the end of the Second World War the theatre and cinema began to feel the effect of television. Its screen could be easily installed at home, thus keeping audiences away from theatre and cinema. And it took variety entertainment almost entirely from the live theatre. Both theatre and cinema were quick to suffer. But because it caters for such a large audience, and has to present so many programmes, there is a tendency for television entertainments to be mundane. This is not to say that all T.V. plays are poor, but obviously, among so many, it is unlikely that more than an occasional one will be very good. Besides, it seems likely that television is at its best with actuality rather than drama. At least drama on television has its own special requirements, which have not yet been fully explored. It is not surprising, then, that the theatre fought back through the playwright. A new group of young writers tried to explore some of the special characteristics of plays written purposely for the live theatre. The play that marked the emergence of the new dramatists was 'Look Back in Anger', by John Osborne, presented at the Royal Court Theatre.

Stephen Joseph, *The Playhouse in England*

74. *True to the Medium****

The large waves roused in the soul bring ashore propositions regarding the significance of the things we fully experience. Films which satisfy our desire for such propositions may well reach into the dimension of ideology. But if they are true to the medium, they will certainly not move from a preconceived idea; conversely, they set out to explore physical data and, taking their cue from them, work their way up to some problem or belief. The cinema is materialistically minded; it proceeds from 'below' to 'above'. The importance of its natural bent for moving in this direction can hardly be overestimated. Indeed, Erwin Panofsky, the great art historian, traces to it the difference between film and the traditional arts; 'The processes of all the earlier representational arts conform, in a higher or lesser degree, to an idealistic conception of the world. These arts operate from bottom to top; they start with an idea to be projected into shapeless matter and not with the objects that constitute the physical world ... It is the movies, and only the movies, that do justice to that materialistic interpretation of the universe which, whether we like it or not, pervades contemporary civilization.'

Guided by film, then, we approach, if at all, ideas no longer on highways leading through the void but on paths that wind through the thicket of things. While the theatregoer watches a spectacle which affects primarily his mind and only through it his sensibility, the moviegoer finds himself in a situation in which he cannot ask questions and grope for answers unless he is saturated physiologically. 'The cinema', says Lucien Seve, ... 'requires of the spectator a new form of activity; his penetrating eye moving from the corporeal to the spiritual'.

S. Kracauer, *Theory of Film*

75. *Sonata Form***

Many a thesis on the subject tends to imply that the Recapitulation is no more than a slavish reprise of the first few pages in which executants and audience alike can go to sleep without risk of missing anything of importance. Nothing could be further from the truth. Many a quickly made friendship has been reconsidered in the light of subsequent knowledge; the whole essence of sonata form as a drama is that the composer presents us with certain material in the Exposition; in the Development we get to know a great deal about it that we have never dreamed of; in the Recapitulation we reassess the material in the light of the experience gained. I cannot overemphasize the importance of the statement. Once we have experienced the Development, once we have learnt the hidden secrets of the characters involved, once we have seen these relationships altered, we can never feel the same about them. In a play, we meet the characters in the first act; as it progresses, our feelings towards them change; new layers of characters are revealed, showing heroism or weakness, treachery or loyalty. Now we know them as people, and by the time they take the curtain call our conception of them can well have altered enormously. The same thing applies to music. A theme is like a living thing; one may find it difficult to feel affection for a tiny stunted clump of green in a flower-bed but once it has grown into a great shrub covered with flowers one's feelings change to a glowing pride.

Anthony Hopkins, Talking about Symphonies

76. *Present Difficulties***

Not all the blame for present difficulties, however, is to be laid at the door of the choralists themselves. We have here a special aspect of today's general gap between public taste and radically modern music. (That a gap of some sort should exist is reasonable; that it should be such a broad gap as at present is disquieting.) It might be validly argued that certain composers today seem to have withdrawn into purely esoteric types of artistic creation which issue no invitation to the intelligent lay listener of the composer's own time. On the other hand, the great majority of today's leading composers have written choral music deliberately suited to actual capabilities of performance, and (as is pointed out in the foregoing chapters) many works written to foreign language texts also have English performing versions available.

Part of the general backwardness of choral activity today is true, paradoxically, to something which is the particular traditional glory of that activity; its close connexion with amateur performance and with social custom and ritual. Choral singing, in our Western-European musical sense, is an art root in the Church. For well over a thousand years the Church has maintained the chief establishments of choral singing—maintained them at an economic cost in order to carry out a well-defined social function. This function links the most diversified activities; Monteverdi composing for St. Mark's in Venice, Bach supplying choirs for five churches in Leipzig, a mid-twentieth-century English schoolmistress acting as village church organist for a few shillings each Sunday. All these social contexts imply an ordered relation between choral music, its performers, and its listeners; all of them imply an ordered choral repertory fitted to prevailing social conditions and prevailing musical skills.

Arthur Jacobs, *Choral Music*

77. *Art and Morality***

Art also has its morality, and many of the rules of this morality are the same as, or at least analogous to, the rules of ordinary ethics. Remorse, for example, is as undesirable in relation to our bad art as it is in relation to our bad behaviour. The badness should be hunted out, acknowledged and, if possible, avoided in the future. To pore over the literary shortcomings of twenty years ago, to attempt to patch a faulty work into the perfection it missed at its first execution, to spend one's middle age in trying to mend the artistic sins committed and bequeathed by that different person who was oneself in youth—all this is surely vain and futile. And that is why this new Brave New World is the same as the old one. Its defects as a work of art are considerable; but in order to correct them I should have to rewrite the book—and in the process of rewriting, as an older, other person, I should probably get rid not only of some of the faults of the story, but also of such merits as it originally possessed. And so, resisting the temptation to wallow in artistic remorse, I prefer to leave both well and ill alone and to think about something else.

Aldous Huxley, *Brave New World*

78. Keats's The Eve of St. Agnes*

The poet, by reference to fragments of a scene, here evokes an image of
a cold winter's night, and every reference to things is as general as the
total image is complete, vivid, precise, and particular. What does the
owl look like? We do not know; it is *an* owl, any owl. The hare limps
trembling through the grass; but there are many ways, even for a hare,
of limping through grass. Numb were the beadsman's fingers; but
apart from numbness what was their physical conformation? Were they
fat or thin, wrinkled or smooth, dirty or clean? The sweet Virgin's
picture is equally general; we supply any we may know of or care to
imagine on the spur of the moment. But from all these objects referred
to in so unparticularized a manner, and to which we each respond with
images fetched from our own recollection, and with varying vividness,
there arises something very particular, a vivid, unified impression or
idea of a cold St. Agnes' Eve which the poet describes to us and which
we all agree about on the basis of his presentation. It is the sort of
description that evokes in early exercises in appreciation the exclama-
tion: the poet makes us *feel* the cold!—though if he really did we might
be less pleased.

Ronald Peacock, The Art of Drama

79. The Nature of Tragedy**

Thus the archetypal pattern corresponding to tragedy may be said to
be a certain organization of the tendencies of self-assertion and submission. The self which is asserted is magnified by that same collective
force to which finally submission is made; and from the tension of the
two impulses and their reaction upon each other, under the conditions
of poetic exaltation, the distinctive tragic attitude and emotion appears
to arise.

The theme of the conflict between the generations considered earlier,
in relation to Hamlet and Orestes, as corresponding to an ambivalent
attitude toward a parent figure—is plainly related to this more general
theme and pattern; since, as we saw, the same underlying emotional
associations cling to the images of father and of king. In experiencing
imaginatively the conflict of the generations, the spectator is identified
with the hero both as son, in his felt solidarity with the father and revolt

against him, and again, when, making reparation for the 'injustice'
against his predecessor, he gives place to a successor, and is reunited
with that whole of life whence he emerged.

Maud Bodkin, *Archetypal Patterns in Poetry*

80. *The Integrity of Poetry****

But if we conceive thus highly of the destinies of poetry, we must also
set our standard for poetry high, since poetry, to be capable of fulfilling
such high destinies, must be poetry of a high order of excellence. We
must accustom ourselves to a high standard and to a strict judgement.
Sainte-Beuve relates that Napoleon one day said, when somebody was
spoken of in his presence as a charlatan: 'Charlatan as much as you
please; but where is there NOT charlatanism?'—'Yes', answers
Sainte-Beuve, 'in politics, in the art of governing mankind, that is
perhaps true. But in the order of thought, in art, the glory, the eternal
honour is that charlatanism shall find no entrance. Herein lies the
inviolableness of that noble portion of man's being.' It is admirably
said, and let us hold fast to it. In poetry, which is thought and art in one,
it is the glory, the eternal honour, that charlatanism shall find no
entrance; that this noble sphere be kept inviolable. Charlatanism is for
confusing and obliterating the distinctions between excellent and
inferior, sound and unsound or only half-sound, true and untrue or
only half-true. It is charlatanism, conscious or unconscious, whenever
we confuse or obliterate these. And in poetry, more than anywhere
else, it is unpermissible to confuse or obliterate them. For in poetry
the distinction between excellent and inferior, sound and unsound or
only half-sound, true and untrue or only half-true, is of paramount
importance.

'The Study of Poetry', *English Critical Texts*, D. J.
Enright and Ernst de Chickera.

81. *Imitation and Originality in Art***

Imitation also is a craft; and therefore a so-called work of art, in so far
as it is imitative, is a work of art falsely so called. At the present time
there is little need to insist on this. Plenty of people paint and write and

compose in a spirit of the purest imitation, and make a name for themselves as painters or writers or musicians solely owing to their success in copying the manner of someone whose reputation is assured; but both they and their public know that in so far as their work is of this kind it is a sham, and it would be a waste of our time to prove it. The opposite thesis would be better worth developing. Originality in art, meaning lack of resemblance to anything that has been done before, is sometimes nowadays regarded as an artistic merit. This, of course, is absurd. If the production of something deliberately designed to be like existing works of art is mere craft, equally so, and for the same reason, is the production of something designed to be unlike them. There is a sense in which any genuine work of art is original; but originality in that sense does not mean unlikeness to other works of art. It is a name for the fact that this work of art is a work of art and not anything else.

R. G. Collingwood, *The Principles of Art*

Section 7. NATURE

82. The Farm**

The woods gave sanctuary to the weary, and there was music in the cool rustle of the leaves in summer, and shelter beneath the naked branches even in winter. She was hungry for birds; and for their flight amongst the trees. She yearned for the homely murmurs of a farm; the cluck of hens, and clarion screech of a cock, and the flustered rasp of geese. She wanted to smell again the rich, warm dung in the sheds, and feel the warm breath of cows upon her hands, heavy footsteps treading the yard, and the clank of pails beside the well. She wanted to lean against a gate and look upon a village lane, give good night to a passing friend, and see the blue smoke curl from the chimneys. There would be voices she would know, rough and gentle in her ear, and a laugh somewhere from a kitchen window. She would concern herself with the business of her farm; rise early and draw water from the well, move amongst her little flock with confidence and ease, bend her back to labour and count the strain a joy and an antidote to pain. All seasons could be welcome for the harvest they should bring, and there would be peace and contentment in her mind. She belonged to the soil, and would return to it again, rooted to the earth as her forefathers had been. Helford had given her birth, and when she died she would be part of it once more.

Daphne du Maurier, *Jamaica Inn*

83. The Segre Valley**

The Segre valley is one of the loveliest in the Pyrenees. True, it is not continually magnificent, but it charms by its contrasts. In many places green slopes or forest-covered ridges drop almost sheer to the river's edge; then, following a rocky gorge, the valley widens to admit fields of chocolate covered earth. The very occasional hamlets fit the scene;

some prefer the hilltop; failing that, the slopes of the mountain, for any level land in the valley is sacred to cultivation.

Now the scene becomes more dramatic. Huge red crags overhang the road, their rocks weathered into fantastic shapes. For stretches of many miles there are no houses in the valley, but an infrequent village perches dizzily on the heights, its means of access seldom visible. Then another upland plain awaited me, with a broad canopy of black cloud and a scent of thunder. I spurred George to unusual efforts, and dashed into Seo de Urgel as the storm broke in violent cataclysms of sound and torrent.

Bernard Newman, *Both Sides of the Pyrenees*

84. The Glacier**

'A little snow can be seen amongst the peaks and gullies opposite to us, and here and there the sparkling white of some hanging glacier is in marked contrast to the rich tones of the bare rock.'

'We are camped in the medial moraine, a long scattered line of boulders of every form and colour. Looking east one can see this line winding down with graceful curves over the blue surface of the glacier, towards the sea; far away beyond is the ice-covered sea itself, pearly grey in the distance. One can follow this highway of boulders to the west too, till it vanishes over the undulating inclines above us; in this direction the glacier wears a formidable aspect, for in its centre is an immense cascade. It is exactly as though this was some river which had suddenly frozen in its course, with the cascade to show where its waters had been dashing wildly over a rocky shallow; it is very beautiful, with its gleaming white waves and deep blue shadows, but we shall have to give it a wide berth when we travel upward. The upper valley is perhaps our most beautiful view; the dark cliffs form a broad V and frame the cascading glacier, and above it the distant solitary peak of the Knob Head Mountain and a patch of crimson sky.'

Captain Robert F. Scott, *The Voyage of the 'Discovery'*

85. No Sentimentality***

He had crossed the fields, passed the little cottages of Seatoller and the yews, and started up the hill to Honister. On the left of him Hause Gill tumbling in miniature cataracts with the recent rain, on the right of him the ever-opening fells. He drew great gulps of air into his lungs. That was for him, that unenclosed fell. As soon as he reached a point where the moss ran unbroken to the sky all his troubles dropped away from him and he was a man. There was no place in the world for open country like this stretch of ground in Northern England and Scotland, for it was man's country; it was neither desert nor icy waste; it had been on terms with man for centuries and was friendly to man. The hills were not so high that they despised you; their rains and clouds and becks and heather and bracken, gold at a season, green at a season, dun at a season, were yours; the air was fresh with kindliness, the running water sharp with friendship, and when the mist came down it was as though the hill put an arm round you and held you even though it killed you. For kill you it might. There was no sentimentality here. It had its own life to lead, and, as in true friendship, kept its personality. It had its own tempers with the universe and, when in a rolling rage, was not likely to stop and inquire whether you chanced to be about or no. Its friendship was strong, free, unsentimental, breathing courage and humour. And the fell ran from hill to hill, springing to the foot, open to the sky, cold to the cheek, warm to the heart, unchanging in its fidelity. As he breasted the hill and turned back to look across Borrowdale the sky began to break.

Hugh Walpole, Rogue Herries

86. The Stream**

There must be a stream there, we reasoned, and went nearer. The sight that met us when we reached the steep rock above the grove, however, enchanted and amazed us. A glittering, crystal-clear stream flowed along under the rock and ran down through a walled channel into a large, square basin, shaded by tall trees. Round the basin peasant girls were kneeling washing clothes, but the materials spread out in the sun were not ordinary factory-made ones but thick woollen coverlets, homespun skirts, rugs, and rags in the most harmonious colours. Pack-donkeys were standing tethered under the trees and an old man was untying more gaily coloured bundles; all the winter woollens of a large farm were evidently being washed. Beyond the basin was a whirring and splashing noise and we found that the water went on down through a thick perpendicular pipe to a small mill on the next shelf. Here, too, donkeys were tethered under the trees and the old miller, covered with white flour dust, was peering out through a hole in the wall.

Göran Schildt, *In the Wake of Odysseus*

87. *Torrents****

The Alps, even, have many a slender stream, perhaps bearing no name, and certainly known by no names out of sight of their nearest peaks, that are remembered in their solitude, or at least remembered at each return of the traveller, where they drop, hushed by their distance as much as by the noisy train. There is one, for instance, seen for but a moment, that has so long a fall as to grow weak and to swing in all the light winds. The strong stem of the cascade springs from the bed of its upland stream; and as from a strong stem a sapling wavers upwards, entangled at last in all breezes, so the dropping brook wavers downwards to its last and lightest motion.

Waterfalls that have turned to torrents have not been so much the subject of the landscape of convention. Their wildness did not take the general fancy when conventions were made; but they are the vitality of the mountains. Theirs is an expression of movement so great that all the Alpine region seems to manifest its life only by these noisy valleys. All communications, all signals and messages of the range, hasten in and out by these brilliant cataracts, one in the depth of every ravine.

They are not only the traffic and mission of their mountains, the coursing of that cold blood and the pulse of the rock, but they carry the mountain spirit far out. There is no country under mountains but has its quietness awakened by wilder rivers than other lands are watered by. When the range is out of sight, the torrents are still hasty, cataract below cataract, shallow and clear, quick from the impulse of waterfalls. No loitering rivers in earthy beds keep level banks in those plains that have their horizon lifted by the line of great mountains.

Alice Meynell, *Waterfalls*

88. *New Life****

In the reedy edges of the inner waters the mallards nested and brought out their young flotillas, muskrats dug communities and swam lithely in the early morning. The ospreys hung, aimed, plummeted on fish, and seagulls carried clams and scallops high in the air and dropped them to break them open for eating. Some otters still clove the water like secret furry whispers; rabbits poached in the gardens and grey squirrels moved like little waves in the streets of the village. Cock pheasants flapped and coughed their crowing. Blue herons poised in the shallow water like leggy rapiers and at night the bitterns cried out like lonesome ghosts.

Spring is late and summer late at New Baytown, but when it comes it has a soft, wild, and special sound and smell and feeling. In early June the world of leaf and blade and flowers explodes, and every sunset is different. Then in the evening the bobwhites state their crisp names and after dark there is a wall of sound of whip-poor-will. The oaks grow fat with leaf and fling their long-tasselled blossoms in the grass. Then dogs from various houses meet and go on picnics, wandering bemused and happy in the woods, and sometimes they do not come home for days.

In June man, hustled by instinct, mows grass, riddles the earth with seeds, and locks in combat with mole and rabbit, ant, beetle, bird, and all others who gather to take his garden from him. Woman looks at the curling-edge petals of a rose and melts a little and sighs, and her skin becomes a petal and her eyes are stamens.

John Steinbeck, *The Winter of Our Discontent*

89. Rain***

Rain, not of gold, swept suddenly across the Tungabhadra river and over the city. We took shelter up a rock slope behind the main street, in the recesses of an unfinished gateway of rough-hewn stone. A very thin man followed us there. He was wrapped in a thin white cotton sheet, dappled with wet. He let the sheet fall off his chest to show us that he was all skin and bones, and he made the gestures of eating. I paid no attention. He looked away. He coughed; it was the cough of a sick man. His staff slipped from his hand and fell with a clatter on the stone floor down which water was now pouring. He hoisted himself on to a stone platform and let his staff lie where it had fallen. He withdrew into the angle of the platform and wall and was unwilling to make any motion, to do anything that might draw attention to himself. The dark gateway framed light; rain was grey over the pagoda-ed city of stone. On the grey hillside, shining with water, there were the marks of quarryings. When the rain was over the man climbed down, picked up

his wet staff, wrapped his sheet about him and made as if to go. I had
converted fear and distaste into anger and contempt; it plagued me like
a wound.

V. S. Naipaul, *An Area of Darkness*

90. *The Call of Farming****

All the same, he was not doing what he wanted to do; the son of a
farmer, he had from the beginning aimed at operating a property of his
own. Facing up to it, he resigned as a county agent after four years and,
on land leased with borrowed money, created, in embryo, River Valley
Farm (a name justified by the Arkansas River's meandering presence
but not, certainly, by any evidence of valley). It was an endeavour that
several Finney County conservatives watched with show-us amusement—
old-timers who had been fond of baiting the youthful county agent on
the subject of his university notions; 'That's fine, Herb. You always
know what's best to do on the other fellow's land. Plant this. Terrace
that. But you might say a sight different if the place was your own.'
They were mistaken; the upstart's experiments succeeded—partly
because, in the beginning years, he laboured eighteen hours a day. Set-
backs occurred—twice the wheat crop failed, and one winter he lost
several hundred head of sheep in a blizzard, but after a decade Mr.
Clutter's domain consisted of over eight hundred acres owned outright
and three thousand more worked on a rental basis—and that, as his
colleagues admitted, was 'a pretty good spread'. Wheat, maize seed,
certified grass seed—these were the crops the farm's prosperity depended upon. Animals were also important—sheep, and especially
cattle. A herd of several hundred Hereford bore the Clutter brand,
though one would not have suspected it from the scant contents of the
livestock corral, which was reserved for ailing steers, a few milking
cows, Nancy's cats, and Babe, the family favourite—an old fat work-
horse who never objected to lumbering about with three or four children astride her broad back.

Truman Capote, *In Cold Blood*

91. *The Tide****

The sun had not yet risen. The sea was indistinguishable from the sky,
except that the sea was slightly creased as if a cloth had wrinkles in it.

Gradually as the sea whitened a dark line lay on the horizon dividing
the sea from the sky and the grey cloth became barred with thick strokes
moving, one after another, beneath the surface, following each other,
pursuing each other, perpetually.

As they reached the shore each bar rose, heaped itself, broke and
swept a thin veil of white water across the sand. The wave paused
and then drew out again, sighing like a sleeper whose breath comes and
goes unconsciously. Gradually the dark bar on the horizon became clear
as if the sediment in an old wine-bottle had sunk and left the glass
green. Behind it, too, the sky cleared as if the white sediment there had
sunk, or as if the arm of a woman couched beneath the horizon had
raised a lamp and flat bars of white, green and yellow spread across the
sky like the blades of a fan. Then she raised her lamp higher and the air
seemed to become fibrous and to tear away from the green surface
flickering and flaming in red and yellow fibres like the smoky fire that
roars from a bonfire. Gradually the fibres of the burning bonfire were
fused into one haze, one incandescence which lifted the weight of the
woollen grey sky on top of it and turned it to a million atoms of soft
blue. The surface of the sea slowly became transparent and lay rippling
and sparkling until the dark stripes were almost rubbed out.

Virginia Woolf, *The Waves*

92. *The Cranes Return****

I turned for a moment and could see the little shepherd who was so
tired of his solitude still standing on his stone. His curly hair, escaping
from under his black handkerchief, was waving in the southern wind.
The light streamed over him from head to foot. I felt I was looking at a
bronze statue of a youth. He had placed his crook across his shoulders
and was whistling.

I took another track and went down towards the coast. Now and then,
warm breezes laden with perfume reached me from nearby gardens. The
earth had a rich smell, the sea was rippling with laughter, the sky was
blue and gleaming like steel.

Winter shrivels up the mind and body of man, but then there comes
the warmth which swells the breast. As I walked I suddenly heard loud
trumpetings in the air. I raised my eyes and saw a marvellous spectacle
which had always moved me deeply since my childhood; cranes de-
ploying across the sky in battle order, returning from wintering in a
warmer country, and, as legend has it, carrying swallows on their wings
and in the deep hollows of their bony bodies.

The unfailing rhythm of the seasons, the ever-turning wheel of life, the four facets of the earth which are lit in turn by the sun, the passing of life—all these filled me once more with a feeling of oppression. Once more there sounded within me, together with the cranes' cry, the terrible warning that there is only one life for all men, that there is no other, and that all that can be enjoyed must be enjoyed here. In eternity no other chance will be given to us.

Nikos Kazantzakis, *Zorba The Greek*

93. *With No Wind****

And now? He stood looking down at the river as it flowed through the quiet land. And something in the still, shining surface of it brought back to him a thing that he had forgotten for more than thirty years. Once when he was a youngster he had gone with his father on pilgrimage to St. Gildas de Rhuis. It was a quiet, shining day with no wind and standing on those terrible cliffs above the point and looking westward, he had seen a strange silver pathway that swept round the headland and out to sea, with no ripple upon it, counter to all the restless fleeing and pursuing of the blue gay-crested waves. His father had stood beside him, so withdrawn into himself that for a long time he had not liked to question him; and when he did, Berengar had answered heavily, with his eyes still upon it, 'It is the will of God'. At supper in the guest house, the old brother that waited upon them spoke of the strong current that swept round the coast and was the terror of all the craft that made for home; and yet it had suffered St. Gildas to float upon it without oar or sail, and landed him unbroken in his coracle in the cove where his image stood. He saw it now, looking down into the valley, as though the river had transformed itself into that swift current, radiant, implacable and strong, and the green fields into the jabble of the tumbling waves. Well, it had brought his father to a quiet haven; it was to take himself to sea.

Helen Waddell, *Peter Abelard*

94. *Fire***

Smoke was rising here and there among the creepers that festooned the dead or dying trees. As they watched, a flash of fire appeared at the

root of one wisp, and then the smoke thickened. Small flames stirred at
the bole of a tree and crawled away through leaves and brushwood,
dividing and increasing. One patch touched a tree trunk and scrambled
up like a bright squirrel. The smoke increased, sifted, rolled outwards.
The squirrel leapt on the wings of the wind and clung to another standing tree, eating downwards. Beneath the dark canopy of leaves and
smoke the fire laid hold on the forest and began to gnaw. Acres of black
and yellow smoke rolled steadily towards the sea. At the sight of the
flames and the irresistible course of the fire, the boys broke into shrill,
excited cheering. The flames, as though they were a kind of wild life,
crept as a jaguar creeps on its belly towards a line of birch-like saplings
that fledged an outcrop of the pink rock. They flapped at the first of the
trees, and the branches grew a brief foliage of fire. The heart of flame
lept nimbly across the gap between the trees and then went swinging
and flaring along the whole row of them. Beneath the capering boys a
quarter of a mile square of forest was savage with smoke and flame. The
separate noises of the fire merged into a drum-roll that seemed to shake
the mountain.

William Golding, Lord of The Flies

95. *Building a Camp***

It took two days of cutting and levelling to get the camp site ready, and
on the third day Smith and I stood on the edge of the grass field watching
while thirty sweating, shouting Africans hauled and pulled at what
appeared to be the vast, brown, wrinkled carcase of a whale that lay on
the freshly turned earth. Gradually as this sea of canvas was pulled and
pushed, it rose into the air, swelling like an unhealthy puffball. Then it
seemed to spread out suddenly, leech-like, and turned itself into a
marquee of impressive dimensions. When it had thus revealed its
identity, there came a full throated roar, a mixture of astonishment,
amazement and delight, from the crowd of villagers who had come to
watch our camp building.

Once the marquee was ready to house us, it took another week of
hard work before we were ready to start collecting. Cages had to be
erected, ponds dug, various chiefs from nearby villages interviewed and
told of the animals we required, food supplies had to be laid on, and a
hundred and one other things had to be done. Eventually when the
camp was functioning smoothly, we felt we could start collecting in

earnest. We had decided that Smith should stay in Mamfe and keep
the base camp going, gleaning what forest fauna he could with the help
of the local inhabitants, while I was to travel further inland.

Gerald Durrell, The Bafut Beagles

96. *Changing Views of Nature***

St. Anselm, writing at the beginning of the twelfth century, maintained
that things were harmful in proportion to the number of senses which
they delighted, and therefore rated it dangerous to sit in a garden where
there are roses to satisfy the senses of sight and smell, and songs and
stories to please the ears. This, no doubt, expresses the strictest monas-
tic view. The average layman would not have thought it wrong to
enjoy nature; he would simply have said that nature was not enjoyable.
The fields meant nothing but hard work (today agricultural labourers
are almost the only class of the community who are not enthusiastic
about natural beauty); the sea coast meant danger of storm and piracy.
And beyond these more or less profitable parts of the earth's surface
stretched an interminable area of forest and swamp. Mr. Aldous
Huxley once observed that if Wordsworth had been familiar with
tropical forests he would have taken a less favourable view of his god-
dess. There is, as he says, something in the character of great forests
which is foreign, appalling, and utterly inimical to intruding life. No
wonder that the few references to nature in the early epics, the sagas
and Anglo-Saxon poetry, are brief and hostile or dwell on its horrors, as
in the description of Grendel's Mere in Beowulf, where the poet sets
out to make us share his terror.

Kenneth Clark, Landscape into Art

Section 8. PEOPLE

97. Profile**

He waited now with the side of his face to me, looking down. In profile his face was sadder than it appeared full-faced; his jaw was humped forward ponderously at the mouth, as if speech would be a weight to him. He was tall, and his waist and chest were thick, straight up from his hips to his armpits, where suddenly his body swelled into broad tight shoulders. His head, his short neck, his shoulders, were all packed protectively together, and protective too was the way the features of his face seemed to merge into one another, without abruptness, like a rolling landscape; one felt that his emotions would be concealed in the hollows of his face, not revealed in the small eyes or the small rounded nose, or the lips that were set forward firmly and roundly around his closed mouth. His skin was bad, and under the brown outer skin there lay limp lumps of flesh along the line of the jaw, under the ears, on either side of the nose. His cheeks were large and his forehead was large and both were scarred, like his protuberant jaw, again and again by his half-secret ailment, making his face, drooping down now, more difficult to read.

Dan Jacobson, *A Dance in the Sun*

98. A Woman of Sixty**

None of that stock died before eighty, or lost their health before they died. She could not be much more than sixty, Laura calculated. She had been married at seventeen to her middle-aged bridegroom, her eldest son was a little over forty. By now she might have been an ugly and weakly old woman. Her neck had been round and white, but now the flesh had shrunk away under her chin and her neck was a narrow fluted tube, and her face was like a mask of stretched hide stuck on top of it. She did not look only ugly and old, she looked poor, like the women in the slums between Radnage Square and the Fulham Road.

Her hair had lost its colour and its lustre. It might not have been washed or brushed for a long time. Her eyes, which had been heavy-lidded and almost vacuously serene, stared anxiously out of deep sockets, as if she were wondering where the rent would come from. She must be got away at once, back to Radnage Square, fed on butter and cream and allowed to rest and given a chance to swim at the Bath Club. She would soon be all right. She was so very strong. It was all a question of getting her out of this apartment.

Rebecca West, *The Birds Fall Down*

99. *In Her Early Fifties***

She was a woman in her early fifties, but she had worn well. She was slender, but wiry, not delicate. She had never been so beautiful, so I had heard, perhaps not even pretty, and it was possible that her looks, which in middle-age suggested that she had once been lovely, were now at their best. She had a dashing, faintly monkey-like attractiveness, the air of a woman who had always known that she was attractive to men. As she herself was fond of saying, 'Once a beauty, always a beauty', by which she didn't mean that the flesh was permanent, but that the confidence which underlay it was. Her great charm, in fact, was the charm of confidence. She was not conceited, though she liked showing off. She knew, she was too worldly not to know, that some men were frightened away. But for many she had an appeal, and she had not doubted it since she was a child.

She was wearing a sunblaze of diamonds on her left shoulder. I looked a little apologetically at my wife, who had put on my latest present, a peridot brooch. Margaret's taste did not run to ostentation, but face to face with Diana, she would not have minded a little more.

The curious thing was that the two of them came from the same sort of family. Diana's father was a barrister, and her relatives, like Margaret's were academics, doctors, the upper stratum of professional people.

C. P. Snow, *Corridors of Power*

100. *Emma Inch****

Emma Inch looked no different from any other middle-aged, thin woman you might glance at in the subway or deal with across the counter of some small store in a country town, and then forget forever. Her hair was drab and unabundant, her face made no impression upon you, her voice I don't remember—it was just a voice. She came to us with a letter of recommendation from some acquaintance who knew that we were going to Martha's Vineyard for the summer and wanted a cook. We took her because there was nobody else, and she seemed all right. She had arrived at our hotel in Forty-fifth Street the day before we were going to leave and we got her a room for the night, because she lived way uptown somewhere. She said she really ought to go back and give up her room, but I told her I'd fix that.

Emma Inch had a big scuffed brown suitcase with her, and a Boston bull terrier. His name was Feely. Feely was seventeen years old and he grumbled and growled and snuffled all the time, but we needed a cook and we agreed to take Feely along with Emma Inch, if she would take care of him and keep him out of the way. It turned out to be easy to keep Feely out of the way because he would lie grousing anywhere Emma put him until she came and picked him up again. I never saw him walk. Emma had owned him, she said, since he was a pup. He was all she had in the world, she told us, with a mist in her eyes. I felt embarrassed but not touched. I didn't see how anybody could love Feely.

I didn't lose any sleep about Emma Inch and Feely the night of the day they arrived, but my wife did. She told me next morning that she had lain awake a long time thinking about the cook and her dog because she felt kind of funny about them.

James Thurber, Vintage Thurber

101. *Portrait of a Film Director****

The image is clear enough: it might be summed up in the title of one of the books devoted to him; 'John Huston: King Rebel.' In many a columnist's fantasy John Huston walks tall (which is undeniable), a rollicking, rumbustious figure out of cinematic Hemingway, hard-riding, hard-drinking, hell-raising, a white hunter with, quite possibly, a black heart. Well, it is a nice, colourful picture, always good for lively copy. But even to see the films which this alleged extravagant, unthinking extrovert has made through the years might give one pause. The Red Badge of Courage? Moby Dick? Freud? Reflections in a Golden Eye? The man who made those things might be many things, but uncomplicated hearty he could never be, never have been.

Nor is the John Huston one may (if one is lucky) meet, may (if one is persistent) talk with, anything like that. He is a giant, certainly, but a gentle giant. When working he is quiet, withdrawn, totally immersed in his work. As I watched him recently shooting some scenes for his latest film, a screen version of Hans Koningsberger's novella 'A Walk with Love and Death', in the woods outside Vienna, there was an unfortunate German journalist who kept murmuring hopefully through rain and shine that all he wanted was ten minutes to ask four questions. Eventually one of the publicity staff approached John Huston in what seemed to be a free moment; could he, perhaps . . .? Huston was mildness itself: yes of course, of course, he'd be delighted. But not now, not just now: 'You see, just now it's got so exciting.' And that was precisely what he meant.

John Russell Taylor, John Huston

102. *The Incompetent***

His career was thenceforth one of unbroken shame. He did not drink, he was exactly honest, he was never rude to his employers, yet was everywhere discharged. Bringing no interest to his duties, he brought no attention; his day was a tissue of things neglected and things done amiss; and from place to place and from town to town, he carried the character of one thoroughly incompetent. No man can bear the word applied to him without some flush of colour, as indeed there is no other that so emphatically slams in a man's face the door of self-respect. And to Herrick, who was conscious of talents and acquirements, who looked down upon those humble duties in which he was found wanting, the pain was the more exquisite. Early in his fall, he had ceased to be able to make remittances; shortly after, having nothing but failure to communicate, he ceased writing home; and about a year before this tale begins, turned suddenly upon the streets of San Francisco by a vulgar and infuriated German Jew, he had broken the last bonds of self-respect, and upon a sudden impulse, changed his name and invested his last dollar in a passage on the mail brigantine, the City of Papeete.

R. L. Stevenson and L. Osbourne, The Ebb-Tide

103. *An Englishwoman****

The little heated fuss in the garden had blown over. That was one of the things he definitely remembered on his return to Israel. 'The trouble with you', Freddy had heard himself tell his friends, 'is you blow neither hot nor cold'. Blow cold, blow hot, it had all blown over. Matt drove Barbara back to the convent, and Joanna, cheerfully breezing-down the recently inflamed atmosphere, left the house with them, a bulky parcel of groceries in her arms. She was holding it like a baby. The parcel was not tied with string; it was loosely bundled together in brown paper; one could see portions of a sugar-package, a bag of flour, and a tin of something sticking out of the upper end of the bundle, like an infant's head. Joanna had said that, while the car was out, it would be a chance to take that stuff to someone or other, one of her poor Arab families. Freddy had seen many such bundles of groceries being borne out of houses, at home and abroad, by many such busy Englishwomen, killers of two birds to the stone, all through his life. At home, the Welfare State had done nothing to change their habits. The scene was all the more typical in that Matt had already gone out to the car, thrusting past her, without any attempt to relieve his wife of the bundle; there was no hint of expectation on her part that he should do so. Freddy's aunts and sister, all their school friends and wives of Freddy's school friends had been for ever dashing out of the house to get a place in the car, with breathless parcels of groceries entwined in their arms, while the husbands pushed past them to the driver's seat.

Muriel Spark, *The Mandelbaum Gate*

104. *Judith****

No one needed Judith. She stood listening to the stillness of the house, half-way up the staircase, her fingers on her lip, considering. She was an odd little creature, even as odd little creatures go. She was very small, though made in excellent proportion, save that her red hair, which hung in ringlets, seemed weighty for her head. Her complexion was pale and would always be so: she had the horse-features of all the Herries, prominent nose and cheek-bones. She was, in fact, no beauty, but there was very much character in her bright and challenging eyes, the resoluteness of her mouth. When she smiled she could be very winning. She could also look very impertinent, and, when angry, with her red hair, her pale face, and perfectly balanced, lightly swinging body she could seem a flying fury. She had tiny hands and feet; of these already she was boastfully proud.

She was dressed in a red bodice with silver buttons and a small orange hoop. She wore red shoes. This was her best dress, bought for her in Carlisle on a birthday by David Herries, who alternately loved and hated her. She was supposed to wear this grand dress only on very special occasions; she put it on most days of the week, but although she wore it so often it was as fresh as when it was new. She had, from the first, that gift of being as clean and spotless in all her circumstances as a piece of china. That was a dirty age, but Judith had always a passion for washing; no water was too cold for her; she was so hardy that nothing ever ailed her.

Hugh Walpole, *Judith Paris*

*105. A Man of Sixty****

About seven o'clock on a cold February night in 1924 a man apparently well in his sixties, with a rough beard of indeterminate grey was standing on one leg in front of a shop in the rue de la Glacière, not far from the boulevard Arago, reading a newspaper by the light of the window with the help of one of those large rectangular magnifying glasses used by stamp collectors. He was wearing a shabby black greatcoat which reached well below his knees and a dark peaked cap of a style introduced around 1885, with a chinstrap of which the double flaps were now fastened over the top. Anyone who examined him at close quarters would have noted that every detail of his get-up was 'like nobody else'. His cap was thirty years out of date; his greatcoat was fastened at the collar by two safety-pins linked together in a short chain; the collar of his starched white shirt was frayed like lace so that the lining showed through, and his tie was not so much a tie as a cord barely covered here and there by some worn black material; his baggy trousers hung at least six inches below what tailors call 'the fork'; and one of his boots (which was enormous) was laced with a piece of string which someone had meant to blacken with ink.

If he had pushed his indiscretion even further, the observer would have noticed that a stout piece of string was also doing duty for our hero's belt, and that he wore no underpants. His inner garments were held together by an armoury of safety-pins, like those of an Arab. On each foot he wore two woollen socks, one on top of the other (whence, no doubt, the size of his boots). Turning out the pockets the observer would have discovered the following items of note: an old crust of bread, two lumps of sugar, a sordid mixture of shreds of black tobacco and solidified bread crumbs, and a solid gold watch, which would have arrested his attention.

Henry de Montherlant, *The Bachelors*

106. Naylor***

Naylor was neither very intelligent nor especially likeable, and certainly not very successful, and from the image of looking down knowingly into his Rock Pool, poking it and observing the curious creatures he might stir up, he would derive a pleasant sense of power. Otherwise the only power he got was from his money. He didn't have a great deal, just under a thousand pounds a year over which a trustee mounted guard like a dragon, but he knew how to be handy with it, how to make some people feel he was paying for them, and others, mostly women and artists, that he might be persuaded to. It was the auxiliary motor which enabled him to navigate through life, under a slender canvas of charm and courage, with a certain obstinacy. 'If you have to be lumped, you don't need to be liked', he was fond of saying, and he generally managed to hit back at whoever he was with for something ambitious and stunted in him. His neat appearance emphasized an arrested boyishness in his smooth chestnut good looks. He had pleasant manners which he had learnt at school, while Oxford had fostered, the one through the dons, the other through the undergraduates, two separate veins of pedantry and lechery, which, united when drunk and when sober divided, were the most definite things you noticed about him. Consequently any intimacies into which he entered never ripened, but were nipped off green by his competitiveness, his delight in catching people out or, worse still, perished in one of his amorous pounces.

Cyril Connolly, *The Rock Pool*

107. The Encounter***

He was jerked wide awake by a rustling in the big heap of bracken beside him . . . Something was there, hiding under the bracken . . . He pushed it aside, hoping for a cat like Tinker, and found himself looking straight into the eyes of a little boy of his own age; a dirty little fair-haired boy clothed in brown rags, with skin burnt by sun and wind as golden brown as an acorn. In a paroxysm of shyness the little boy fell flat on his stomach and pulled the bracken over his head, but through it his eyes shone like two bright stars. Diccon also fell flat on his stomach, his head close to the little boy's, and through the dry, sweet-smelling fronds the blue eyes and the green twinkled at each other. Then they began to laugh, wrinkling their noses and kicking their bare legs in the air. They laughed more and more, rolling over each other, pushing the bracken down each other's necks and kicking and squeaking like a couple of puppies. They had come together at last and were ecstatically happy. They had been born in the same hour on the same night, when all the stars were dancing. Their eyes had opened to moonlight and candlelight, heaven and earth shining together in welcome, and the first breaths they took were fragrant breaths that came blowing over the flowery earth. They had drunk the same mother's milk from a gypsy's breast and listened to the same songs crooned in their ears. They were fortunate children, born at full moon in the spring and dowered by the fairies with the gift of laughter, but never so fortunate as at this moment when they found each other.

Elizabeth Goudge, *Towers in the Mist*

*108. An Irish Priest****

I wished to go in and look at him, but I had not the courage to knock. I walked away slowly along the sunny side of the street, reading all the theatrical advertisements in the shop-windows as I went. I found it strange that neither I nor the day seemed in a mourning mood and I felt even annoyed at discovering in myself a sensation of freedom as if I had been freed from something by his death. I wondered at this for, as my uncle had said the night before, he had taught me a great deal. He had studied in the Irish college in Rome and he had taught me to pronounce Latin properly. He had told me stories about the catacombs and about Napoleon Bonaparte, and he had explained to me the meaning of the different ceremonies of the Mass and of the different vestments worn by the priest. Sometimes he had amused himself by putting difficult questions to me, asking me what one should do in certain circumstances or whether such and such sins were mortal or venial or only imperfections. His questions showed me how complex and mysterious were certain institutions of the Church which I had always regarded as the simplest acts. The duties of the priest toward the Eucharist and towards the secrecy of the confessional seemed so grave to me that I wondered how anybody had ever found in himself the courage to undertake them; and I was not surprised when he told me that the fathers of the Church had written books as thick as the Post Office Directory and as closely printed as the law notices in the newspaper, elucidating all these intricate questions. Often when I thought of this I could make no answer or only a very foolish and halting one,

upon which he used to smile and nod his head twice or thrice. Sometimes he used to put me through the responses of the Mass, which he
had made me learn by heart; and, as I pattered, he used to smile
pensively and nod his head, now and then pushing huge pinches of
snuff up each nostril alternately. When he smiled he used to uncover
his big discoloured teeth and let his tongue lie upon his lower lip—a
habit which had made me feel uneasy in the beginning of our acquaintance before I knew him well.

James Joyce, Dubliners

*109. Married by Surprise***

I took a decisive step when I married Antonia. I was then thirty, and
she was thirty-five. She looks now, for all her beauty, a little older than
her years, and she has more than once been taken for my mother. My
real mother, who among other things was a painter, died when I was
sixteen, but at the time of my marriage my father was still alive and I
had hitherto been but casually involved in the wine trade. I was more
concerned, though that also in a dilettante fashion, with being a
military historian, a type of study in which, if I could have brought
myself to abandon my amateur status, I might have excelled. When I
married Antonia, however, everything came, for some time, to a stand-
still. As I say, I was fortunate to get her. Antonia had been, and indeed
still was, a somewhat eccentric society beauty. Her father was a distinguished regular soldier, and her mother, who came out of the
Bloomsbury world, was something of a minor poet and a remote relation of Virginia Woolf. For some reason Antonia never got a sensible
education, though she lived abroad a great deal and speaks three languages fluently; and also, for some reason, and although much courted,
she did not marry young. She moved in a fashionable society, more
fashionable than that which I frequented, and became through her pro-
tracted refusal to marry, one of its scandals. Her marriage to me, when
it came, was a sensation.

Iris Murdoch, A Severed Head

*110. The Great Gatsby****

And, after boasting this way of my tolerance, I came to the admission
that it has a limit. Conduct may be founded on the hard rock or the wet

marshes, but after a certain point I don't care what it's founded on. When I came back from the East last autumn I felt that I wanted the world to be in uniform and at a sort of moral attention forever; I wanted no more riotous excursions with privileged glimpses into the human heart. Only Gatsby, the man who gives his name to this book, was exempt from my reaction—Gatsby, who represented everything for which I have an unaffected scorn. If personality is an unbroken series of successful gestures, then there was something gorgeous about him, some heightened sensitivity to the promises of life, as if he were related to one of those intricate machines that register earthquakes ten thousand miles away. This responsiveness had nothing to do with that flabby impressionability which is dignified under the name of the 'creative temperament'—it was an extraordinary gift for hope, a romantic readiness such as I have never found in any other person and which it is not likely I shall ever find again. No—Gatsby turned out all right at the end; it is what preyed on Gatsby, what foul dust floated in the wake of his dreams that temporarily closed out my interest in the abortive sorrows and shortwinded elations of men.

F. Scott Fitzgerald, *The Great Gatsby*

*III. A Depressing Scene***

Eric walked into the kitchen, which was only slightly less disordered than he now felt himself to be, and put coffee on the stove. He stood there a moment, watching the blue flame in the gloom of the small room. He took down two coffee cups and found the milk and sugar. He returned to the big room and cleared the night table of books and of urgently scrawled notes—nearly all of which, beneath his eyes, as he wrote them on small scraps of paper, had hardened into irrelevance— and emptied the ashtray. He picked up his clothes, and Vivaldo's from the floor, piling them on a chair, and straightened the sheets on the bed. He put the cups and the milk and sugar on the night table, discovered that there were only five cigarettes left, and searched in his pockets for more, but there were none. He was hungry, but the refrigerator was empty. He thought that, perhaps, he could find the energy to dress and run down to the corner delicatessen for something—Vivaldo was probably hungry, too. He walked to the window and peeked out through the blinds. The rain poured down like a wall. It struck the pavement with a vicious sound and spattered in the swollen gutters with the force of bullets. The asphalt was wide and white and blank with rain. The gray pavements danced and gleamed and sloped. Nothing moved, not a car, not a person, not a cat; and the rain was the only sound. He forgot about going to the store, and merely watched the rain, comforted by the anonymity and the violence—this violence was also peace.

James Baldwin, *Another Country*

112. The History of Miss Williams***

My father was an eminent merchant in the city, who, having in the course of trade suffered very considerable losses, retired in his old age, with his wife, to a small estate in the country, which he had purchased with the remains of his fortune. At the time I, being but eight years of age, was left in town for the convenience of education, boarded with an aunt, who was a rigid Presbyterian, and who confined me so closely to what she called the duties of religion, that, in time, I grew weary of her doctrines, and by degrees conceived an aversion for the good books she daily recommended to my perusal. As I increased in age, and appeared with a person not disagreeable, I contracted a good deal of acquaintance among my own sex, one of whom, after having lamented the restraint I was under from the narrowness of my aunt's sentiments, told me I must now throw off the prejudices of opinion imbibed under her influence and example, and learn to think for myself; to which purpose she advised me to read Shaftesbury, Tindal, Hobbes, and all the books which are remarkable for their deviation from the old way of thinking, and, by comparing one with another, I should soon be able to form a system of my own. I followed her advice; and whether it was owing to my prepossession against what I had formerly read, or the clearness of argument in these my new instructors, I know not but I studied them with pleasure, and in a short time became a professed Freethinker.

Smollett, *Roderick Random*

Section 9. HISTORY

*113. The Agricultural Revolution***

The changes so effected have been called in retrospect 'the agricultural revolution', because they worked not by an expansion of an old economic and social system but by the creation of a new one. Great compact estates cultivated in large farms by leasehold tenants employing landless labourers covered more and more of the acreage of England, at the expense of various forms of petty cultivation and ownership. Small squires, and peasants with diminutive rights in the soil were bought out to make room for the new order. The open fields of the great midland corn area were enclosed into the chess-board pattern of fenced fields which has been ever since the hall-mark of the English landscape. And even in the half of England where enclosed fields had always been the rule, analogous social changes were taking place. For everywhere the larger owners were consolidating their estates by purchase; everywhere squires and farmers were busy with new methods. And everywhere better roads, canals and machines were diverting industry from cottage and village to factory and town, thereby cutting off the peasant family from spinning and other small manufacturing activities by which its meagre budget had been eked out.

Taking into account the great variety of local conditions, it is true to say of England as a whole that enclosure was only one, but possibly the most important, of the many changes that combined to reduce the numbers of the independent peasantry, while increasing the aggregate wealth of the countryside.

G. M. Trevelyan, *English Social History*

*114. The Body of St. Isidore***

In December of that year the city of León was the scene of the solemn ceremonies attending the dedication of the new basilica to St. Isidore.

Ferdinand had recently defeated King Motadid of Seville and the terms of the peace he imposed indicate the extent to which Ferdinand and his Leonese subjects were actuated by religious as well as material aims, for, in addition to the usual indemnity, he demanded the remains of Justa, the martyred saint, that they might be transferred to León. As the delegation of bishops sent to Seville were unable to find the remains of the martyr, they took away in their stead those of St. Isidore, 'the Egregious Doctor', whose learned works were in every library in Europe. It should be added that at the head of the Christian delegation was the bishop of León, Alvito, to whom St. Isidore appeared three times and said: 'I am the Doctor of the Spains and mine is the body to be removed.' St. Isidore's body, furthermore, revealed itself to the questing delegation by divine odours, and on the way back to León worked miracles, curing the lame and blind and casting out devils. Wherever the corpse rested at night it was found so heavy the next morning that it could not be moved until the inhabitants promised to found and endow a church on the spot; that done, it miraculously became light and transportable again. Henceforth St. Isidore in his new sepulchre soon won great celebrity for the church and the city of León and became, as a worker of miracles, a serious rival to St. James of Compostella.

Walter Starkie, *The Road to Santiago*

115. Roman Standing Army in Spain*

Cato was awarded a well deserved triumph at Rome, but Spain was very far from settled; year after year the Celtiberians, in the centre of the peninsula (in the modern Castile) and the Lusitanians, in the west and south-west, gave trouble to the governors of the Hither and Further Provinces. In fact it was in Spain that the Romans first maintained a standing army. Originally the burgesses had been called out for each campaign, and the long continued service of the second Punic War had been only an exception, due to the life and death character of the struggle; but it was obviously impossible to change an army every year in a district so remote as Spain. Hence the custom grew up that a Roman might be called upon to serve continuously for sixteen years in the infantry or for ten in the cavalry.

The Spanish service was very unpopular; the risk was great and the booty was small; hence the evil custom of putting unfair burdens on the allied troops was developed, and an undue proportion of them was sent to distant campaigns.

J. Wells, *A Short History of Rome*

116. *Educational Growth***

Outside the schools two problems were growing in intensity during the decade. The first was the relationship of the voluntary schools to the national system, and the second concerned the whole question of educational administration, both local and national.

The rapid extension of the voluntary schools during the 'seventies had placed on the Churches a burden which they found increasingly difficult to carry. They received no aid from the rates, and they earned a slightly smaller grant from the Education Department than the board schools. They were compelled to employ more unqualified teachers, to pay smaller salaries, and to purchase less equipment than their rivals. They were required to put their buildings into repair, to add classrooms and cloakrooms and to bring the sanitation up to more modern standards. They protested that they were being treated unfairly, and demands for further financial assistance were put forward more and more insistently. At a conference called by the Archbishops of Canterbury and York it was agreed to ask the State to pay the whole cost of the teaching staffs of the Church schools, and with the advent of a Conservative Government in 1895 they drafted a Bill embodying this proposal.

Frank Smith, *A History of English Elementary Education*

117. *Demoralization***

The dream was a delusion. There was no prosperity in store for the subjects of the Almoravides. What had happened to the Romans and the Goths now happened to the Berbers. They came to Spain hardy rough warriors, unused to ease or luxuries, delighting in feats of strength and prowess, filled with a fierce but simple zeal for their religion. They had not been long in the enjoyment of the fruits of their victory when all the demoralization which the soft luxuries of Capua brought upon the soldiers of Hannibal came also upon them. They lost their martial habits, their love of deeds of daring, their pleasure in enduring hardships in the brave way of war—they lost all their manliness with inconceivable rapidity. In twenty years there was no Berber army that could be trusted to repel the attacks of the Castilians; in its place was a disorganized crowd of sodden debauchees, miserable poltroons, who had drunk and fooled away their manhood's vigour and become slave to all the appetites that make men cowards. Instead of preserving order, they had now become the disturbers of order; brigands, when they could pluck up courage to attack a peaceful traveller; thieves on all promising opportunities. The country was worse off than ever it had been, even under the rule of petty tyrants. The enfeebled Berbers were at the beck and call of bad women and ambitious priests, and they would counter order one day what they had commanded the day before. Such rulers do not rule for long. A great revolution was sapping the power of the Almoravides in Africa, and the Castilians under Alfonso the Battler resumed their raids into Andalusia.

Stanley Lane Poole, *The Moors in Spain*

118. The King's Anger**

The accusers had little difficulty in poisoning the King's mind. Alphonso lent a ready ear to the false imputations of the meddlers and backbiters and in a paroxysm of rage deprived the Cid of all the castles and towns and every honour he had conferred upon him two years before. He also gave orders for the Cid's own estates to be occupied, his houses to be razed, and all the gold, silver, and other riches that could be found to be confiscated. He even went to the length of subjecting Doña Jimena to the indignity of being bound and cast into prison with her children. Here it should be understood that the materialistic Germanic law, opposed in vain by the Romanized Visigothic code, held the family jointly liable in all penal matters (even a whole neighbourhood was held responsible for the crime of one inhabitant). It followed, therefore, that the wife could be called upon to pay the penalty for her husband's offences. True, in practice, the responsibility was purely pecuniary, and even this custom tended to fall into disuse with the progress of ideas; but in cases of high treason the law was inexorable, condemning to death both the traitor and his family. And that was the position in which Rodrigo came very near to finding himself, for he was accused of conspiring against the King's life. To make matters worse, as the Cid was now without a friend amongst the nobility of Castile, there was no one at all to curb Alphonso's wrath.

Ramón Menéndez Pidal, *The Cid and his Spain*

Appendix

In addition to model translations, the following excerpts from Spanish authors are offered in the hope that they will offer stylistic felicities worthy of imitation.

119. Narrative

En la aldea ocurría algo extraño. La puerta de la empalizada, estaba abierta. Por encima del tejado había parado la luna. En el patio, tres mujeres estaban sentadas en el suelo, en hilera, con los mantos sobre la cabeza y las manos abandonadas en las rodillas. Manos de campesina, ociosas, abandonadas sobre la falda negra. Esto le dio la verdadera sensación de anormalidad. Los pies de Juan Niño se detuvieron. Entonces se dio cuenta de como le estaban mirando las mujeres, el mozo del establo y la luna. ¡Oh, luna quieta! Nadie le había contado a Juan Niño el cuento del viejo que llevaba leña a la luna, pero también a él prendía los ojos, como a todos los niños del mundo. En la puerta de la casa, apareció una de las criadas. Al verle, se tapó la cara como si fuera a llorar. Juan Niño comprendía que debía continuar avanzando, avanzando, hasta que una fuerza ajena y superior se lo impidiera. Cruzó el patio y subió la escalera. En el cuarto de la madre había luz, y en el suelo se recortaba el cuadro amarillo de la puerta. Era una luz especial, una luz con olor, gusto y tacto. No había en ella nada violento ni deslumbrante. Vidriosa y densa, emborronaba la oscuridad como un aliento. Siguió avanzando, menudo y solemne, con los brazos caidos a lo largo del cuerpo. Al cruzar el umbral, su sombra apenas dejaba en el suelo un negro parpadeo. En todo él, había algo de temblor estelar, de hierba azotada.

Ana María Matute, Fiesta al noroeste

The pattern of this passage is determined by the preterite verbs which indicate the successive events of the narrative. With clear cut precision they take us step by step from the patio to the mother's room. Sudden and simple they announce the facts baldly, for instance, 'Los pies de Juan Niño se detuvieron', or 'Cruzó el patio y subió la escalera'. In the longer sentences atmosphere and description are added by means of a wealth of nouns and adjectives.

For pace and control in narrative, the verbs are the key.

SUGGESTED MODELS

Cervantes	*Las novelas ejemplares*
P. A. de Alarcón	*El sombrero de tres picos*
Quevedo	*El Buscón*
Carmen Laforet	*Nada*
M. Aub	*Ciertos cuentos*

120. *Descriptive*

Una franja de color canela solía marcar la frontera entre el agua y la tierra. Más allá comenzaba a brotar la vegetación desigual y asimétrica, en ese desorden caótico y ordenado al propio tiempo con que Dios sabe animar sus propias obras. En ocasiones, cuando el litoral que recortábamos era el del Norte de España, me deleitaba dejando pasar las horas absorto en una muda contemplación. La tierra, en esos casos, adquiría calidades de óptima belleza. El azul y el verde se asociaban en la franja canela divisoria, demostrando al orbe entero que entre los colores cabe una armonía cromática, que ningún color riñe con otro si la tonalidad proviene de las vitales energías que animan espontáneamente la costa de la tierra. Se extendían los bosques, apretados, densos, exuberantes, corriendo ladera abajo hasta detenerse a dos pasos del mar. Bosques de castaños, de eucaliptus, de pinabetes . . . Bosques y bosques a lomos de los prados verdes, formando un tapiz de irisaciones delicadas, donde nada contrastaba briosamente, sino desposeyéndose lenta, paulatinamente, de su coloración particular; fundiéndose, entregándose a la luz común en un mórbido impulso de renuncia hacia la propia forma y la substancia característica.

Miguel Delibes, La sombra del ciprés es alargada

In descriptive writing the rhythm is often tightened, brought to a climax and then gently relaxed to quiescence. In this passage of Miguel Delibes, the technique can be seen at work. A liberal sprinkling of nouns and deliberate restriction of verbs, gives a dignified stateliness to the opening. Gradually the clauses are extended until the climax is reached in the sentence ending ... 'a dos pasos del mar'. Then little by little, the tension is relaxed and, with a backward glance at the word 'Bosques' it comes to rest on the words 'la substancia característica'.

SUGGESTED MODELS

Valera	*Juanita la Larga*
Pardo Bazán	*Los Pazos de Ulloa*
Fernán Caballero	*La gaviota*
Pereda	*Peñas arriba*
A. Palacio Valdés	*José*
Ana María Matute	*Tres y un sueño*
M. Delibes	*El camino*

121. Social Comment

Mi madre no sabía leer ni escribir; mi padre sí, y tan orgulloso estaba de ello que se lo echaba en cara cada lunes y cada martes, y con frecuencia, y aunque no viniera a cuento, solía llamarla ignorante, ofensa gravísima para mi madre, que se ponía como un basilisco. Algunas tardes venía mi padre para casa con un papel en la mano y, quisiéramos que no, nos sentaba a los dos en la cocina y nos leía las noticias; venían después los comentarios y en ese momento yo me echaba a temblar porque estos comentarios eran siempre el principio de alguna bronca. Mi madre, por ofenderlo, le decía que el papel no ponía nada de lo que leía y que todo lo que decía se lo sacaba mi padre de la cabeza, y a éste, el oírla esa opinión le sacaba de quicio; gritaba como si estuviera loco, la llamaba ignorante y bruja y acababa siempre diciendo a grandes voces que si él supiera decir esas cosas de los papeles a buena hora se le hubiera ocurrido casarse con ella. Ya estaba armada. Ella le llamaba desgraciado y peludo, lo tachaba de hambriento y portugués, y él, como si esperara a oír esa palabra para golpearla, se sacaba el cinturón y la corría todo alrededor de la cocina hasta que se hartaba. Yo, al principio, apañaba algún cintarazo que otro, pero cuando tuve más experiencia y aprendí que la única manera de no mojarse es no estando a la lluvia, lo que hacía, en cuanto veía que las cosas tomaban mal cariz, era dejarlos solos y marcharme. Allá ellos.

Camilo José Cela, La familia de Pascual Duarte

With spontaneous simplicity and intuitive insight, the passage portrays a provincial domestic scene. Making no explicit comment, its rebuke is oblique. Pedantry is avoided. The effect is achieved by the use of simple words and concepts. The constructions have the apparent artlessness of an interior monologue. It is an indirect comment upon illiteracy and primitive male pride.

SUGGESTED MODELS

Ciro Bayo	*El Lazarillo Español*
C. J. Cela	*La colmena*
J. M. Gironella	*Un millón de muertos*
M. Ballesteros	*Mi hermano y yo por esos mundos*
M. de Azcárate	*El hombre que no sabía pecar*
M. V. Peña	*La ruta*
M. Barrios	*El crimen*

122. Science

Las investigaciones del ilustre Ramón y Cajal establecieron el principio de la neurona como unidad celular del sistema nervioso. Su hipótesis fue confirmada a principios del siglo con el descubrimiento del impulso nervioso como unidad funcional de la neurona. Dicho impulso se manifiesta a modo de brusco cambio de potencial eléctrico en cierto punto de la neurona y se propaga por ésta a modo de onda de potencial. Su intensidad es independiente del estímulo disparador y posee carácter de 'todo o nada'.

Durante mucho tiempo se tenía la siguiente idea sobre la actividad funcional de las neuronas centrales. En estado normal hay una diferencia de potencial—el potencial de reposo—entre las caras interna y externa de la membrana celular. Los impulsos de interneuronas y receptores períficos son trasmitidos a la neurona central vía sus juntas o sinapsis, y los potenciales de excitación resultantes rebajan la diferencia de potencial a través de la membrana. Al principio esta despolarización se propaga por la superficie celular, que en esta fase se comporta como centro conductor; se habla de una 'propagación electrónica'. Al acentuarse la despolarización la neurona deja de actuar como centro conductor pasivo y finalmente se alcanza cierto umbral. Entonces se inicia el impulso nervioso, llamado potencial de acción o *spike*. De acuerdo con la teoría clásica, el *spike* invade la totalidad de la neurona y, después, siguiendo los terminales del axon, va a estimular otras neuronas.

'Actividad funcional de la neurona de los moluscos.'
Endeavour, Vol. XXV, No. 94, Jan. 1966

Given the technical terms, scientific language is international and simple. Subtract *neurona, estímulo, disparador, receptores períficos, sinapsis, despolarización* and *axon* from this passage and the problem has become simplicity itself.

SUGGESTED MODELS

Many industrial companies publish magazines giving scientific details of their activities. Not all of these magazines are in Spanish but many of them are. The best material is with I.C.I. and Marconi. They can be very generous with their help. *Endeavour*, another I.C.I. venture, is a mine of information. *Industria Británica* is an interesting source.

123. Philosophical

El caso es que, recluído en la estrechez de su campo visual, consigue, en efecto, descubrir nuevos hechos y hacer avanzar su ciencia, que él apenas conoce, y con ella la enciclopedia del pensamiento, que concienzudamente desconoce. ¿Cómo ha sido y es posible cosa semejante? Porque conviene recalcar la extravagancia de este hecho innegable; la ciencia experimental ha progresado en buena parte merced al trabajo de hombres fabulosamente mediocres, y aun menos que mediocres. Es decir, que la ciencia moderna, raíz y símbolo de la civilización actual, da acogida dentro de sí al hombre intelectualmente medio y le permite operar con buen éxito. La razón de ello está en lo que es, a la par, ventaja mayor y peligro máximo de la ciencia nueva y de toda la civilización que ésta dirige y representa; la mecanización. Una buena parte de las cosas que hay que hacer en física y en biología es faena mecánica de pensamiento que puede ser ejecutada por cualquiera, o poco menos. Para los efectos de innumerables investigaciones es posible dividir la ciencia en pequeños segmentos, encerrarse en uno y desentenderse de los demás. La firmeza y exactitud de los métodos permiten esta transitoria y práctica desarticulación del saber. Se trabaja con uno de esos métodos como una máquina, y ni siquiera es forzoso para obtener abundantes resultados poseer ideas rigorosas sobre el sentido y fundamento de ellos. Así la mayor parte de los científicos empujan el progreso general de la ciencia encerrados en la celdilla de su laboratorio; como la abeja en su panal o como el pachón de asador en su cajón.

José Ortega y Gasset, *La rebelión de las masas*

Here the vocabulary is simple. In contrast with many philosophers Ortega y Gasset makes his ideas plain by avoiding technical jargon and crystalizing his concepts. Words ending in *-ión*, *-miento*, *-eza* and *-tud* are frequent. In such writing they only add to the clarity. Ornamental writing, except for pertinent comparisons, is avoided. The idea is the thing.

SUGGESTED MODELS

Ortega y Gasset	*La rebelión de las masas*
Ángel Ganivet	*Idearium español*
M. de Unamuno	*Del sentimiento trágico de la vida*
J. María Pemán	*Novelas y cuentos*
G. Marañón	*Antonio Pérez*
R. Maeztu	*La crisis del humanismo*

124. The Arts

No sólo de este modo material colaboraba el Rey en la obra de su arquitecto, sino que uno de los méritos de éste fue interpretar en la austera sequedad y en la inflexible corrección clásica de las severas líneas del monumento, el pensamiento de su fundador. El momento, por otra parte, era propicio para una reacción de Arquitectura en sentido clásico, después de la pujanza con que se abrió paso el Renacimiento y de la exuberancia decorativa con que se prodigó el estilo plateresco en tiempos de Carlos V. Los días de Felipe II son de lucha por la idea religiosa y por el poderío del vasto imperio del César, lucha que su sucesor afronta con inflexible voluntad y meditado juicio acogiéndose a la oración y al cálculo. Son días de crisis en el arte. Sus grandes luminares del Renacimiento se habían eclipsado; a su fuerza creadora había sustituido el perfeccionamiento técnico. Educado en él y en las clásicas doctrinas de Vignola, Juan de Herrera en el Escorial hace una obra maestra de construcción y sin recursos decorativos, que debió vedarle el Rey, hace un monasterio-panteón donde en medio de la grandeza monumental el espíritu se encuentre forzado a meditar en lo efímero de la vida terrena; extraña cosa producir con elementos clásicos la sensación del despego de lo mundano; sensación que habían expresado con espiritual grandeza los monumentos de la Edad Media.

Escorial, *El arte en España*

Like so many commentaries on the arts, the style smacks of the study rather than the studio. It is erudite, self conscious, perhaps even pompous. Words like *doctrina*, *monasterio-panteón*, *elementos clásicos* and *luminares del Renacimiento* become part of the trade. So away with spontaneity and bring out the *voces cultas*, unless like Azorín there is the chance to create atmosphere.

SUGGESTED MODELS

Menéndez y Pelayo	*Historia de las ideas estéticas*
Azorín	*Al margen de los clásicos*
Gómez de la Serna	*Goya*
Guías Artísticas de España	*Madrid, Valencia, etc.*

Blanco y Negro has frequent articles on ceramics, monuments, parks, and towns.

125. Nature

A primer golpe diríase una tierra juvenil, viéndola vestida de verdura y envuelta en frescor; pero no es así, sino tierra vieja, o madura y adulta si se quiere. Apenas se descubre, sino a muy largos trechos, las entrañas berroqueñas de la tierra, ni la roca aflora el suelo. Aguas seculares han tenido tiempo de desgastar y pulir los desgarrones del terreno; las esquinosas sierras, tal como surgen de las roturas y levantamientos, se han ido hundiendo y desmoronando en montes terrosos y chatos, de contornos ondulantes y sinuosos, como de senos y caderas mujeriles, a la vez que se han ido rellanando los valles y vagueras. El esqueleto de la tierra hase ocultado bajo la carne mollar, sin que asomen juanetes ni pómulos de escualidez. Y luego la frondosa cabellera de castaños, pinos, robles, olmos y cien otras castas de árboles, cubriendo aquellas redondeces y turgencias, dan al paisaje un marcado carácter femenino. Y como tal atrae a sus brazos y llama a reclinarse en reposo en su regazo, a soñar en las haldas de sus montes; es un paisaje habitable, que seduce como un nido incubador de morriñas y *saudades*; es una naturaleza humanizada, hecha mansión del hombre, lugar de descanso en que os aduerme como caricia tibia un aliento de humedad y las quejumbres dulces de los pinos. Y en este paisaje que convida al reposo y al ensueño, hay que luchar rudamente y en despejo de vela para poder vivir y arrancarle el sustento y mantenerle para que mantenga. Es un país femenino.

Miguel de Unamuno, *Por tierras de Portugal y de España*

The vocabulary of nature in itself has sufficient overtones of meaning to spark off an immediate response. And *verdura, frescor, entrañas berroqueñas, desgarrones del terreno, redondeces, robles* and *pinos* are no exceptions. They still have force, though Unamuno keeps them well documented, codified and arranged as though on orderly display in a museum. In passages like these, get the vocabulary right and nature will speak for you.

SUGGESTED MODELS

C. J. Cela	*Viaje a la Alcarria*
M. Delibes	*Por esos mundos*
J. Goytisolo	*Campos de Níjar*
M. de Unamuno	*Por tierras de Portugal y de España*
G. A. Bécquer	*Desde mi celda*
P. Baroja	*Fantasías vascas*

126. People

Jaro, velloso, enjuto, chiquitín, más tieso que un naipe, más duro que un acero, la cara fosca, el hocico de zorro, los ojuelos grises, erizado el bigote, lo mismo que el tupé, roja y puntiaguda la nariz, el cuello erguido, arqueadas las piernas y la cabeza para atrás, con un aire despreciativo y socarrón de huraño y perdonavidas, era don Francisco Sánchez Albarracín, más conocido y popular por 'el doctor Albarracín', uno de los primeros operadores del Instituto Valdés.

Además de insigne cirujano, era el doctor Albarracín, dentro y fuera de su profesión, uno de los tipos más pintorescos, ingeniosos, mordaces y atrabiliarios que pude conocer en este mundo. Lleno de púas como un puerco espín, manojo de nervios en constante irritación, lengua de víbora en perpetua acritud, eterno disidente de todo lo humano y lo divino, rebelde y hostil a toda ley, razón o autoridad, oposicionista rabioso, contradictor desapacible, reñido hasta con su sombra, no sabía sino hablar muy recio, toser muy bronco, sonarse a trompetazos, reir a carcajadas, discutir a voces, argumentar a puños, y sólo consecuente en esto, en lo desaforado y estrepitoso, pues era en todo lo demás una paradoja andante, diz que soñaba a gritos, dormía a vuelcos y roncaba como un león.

Ricardo León, El hombre nuevo

Apart from suitable vocabulary, available in any well ordered selection, comparisons, similes, adjectives and ironical comment help to make descriptions agreeably acceptable. In this passage, 'más tieso que

un naipe', 'como un puerco espín', and 'roncaba como un león', are
acceptable gambits.

SUGGESTED MODELS

Quevedo	*El Buscón*
V. Blasco Ibáñez	*Cañas y barro*
B. Pérez Galdós	*Fortunata y Jacinta*
J. M. Gironella	*Un hombre*
J. A. Payno	*El curso*
A. Palacio Valdés	*La historia de un novelista*

127. History

Eran hasta quinientos hombres de guerra, y al frente de ellos Cemaco,
su cacique, hombre resuelto y tenaz, dispuesto a defender su tierra a
todo trance contra aquella nube de advenedizos. Temieron los españoles
el éxito de la batalla, y encomendándose al cielo, ofrecieron, si con-
seguían la victoria, dar al pueblo que edificasen en aquel país el nombre
de Santa María de la Antigua, una imagen en Sevilla de gran venera-
ción. Hizo además Enciso jurar a todos mantener su puesto a muerte o
a vida sin volver la espalda, y hechas estas prevenciones, dio la señal de
la batalla. Levantan al instante el grito, y con ímpetu terrible se arrojan
sobre los indios, que con no menor ánimo los recibieron. Pero los
españoles pelearon como desesperados, y las armas desiguales con que
combatían no dejaron durar mucho tiempo la refriega, que fue terminada
con el estrago y la fuga de los salvajes despavoridos. Los españoles,
alegres con su triunfo, entraron en el pueblo, donde hallaron muchas
preseas de oro fino y abundancia de provisiones y ropas de algodón.
Corrieron después la tierra, hallaron en los cañaverales del río todos los
efectos preciosos que los indios habían allí ocultado; y hechos cautivos
los pocos que no pudieron escapar, sentaron tranquilamente su domi-
nación. Envió en seguida Enciso por los españoles que había dejado en
la banda oriental del golfo, y todos contentos y esperanzados se pusieron
a fundar la villa, que según el voto hecho antes de la batalla se llamó
Santa María de la Antigua del Darién.

M. J. Quintana, *La vida de Vasco Núñez de Balboa*

The pace of the narrative is emphasized by the positioning of the
verbs. 'Eran hasta quinientos hombres', sets the subject of the para-
graph. Identity is established. From then on their deeds are expressed

in verbs many of which head the sentence they introduce ... 'Temieron los españoles'. There is a matter of fact atmosphere, which helps the author in his recreation of historical fact. To emulate the style attention to word order and the choice of vocabulary are the essential requirements.

SUGGESTED MODELS

G. Marañón	*Antonio Pérez*
F. Díaz Plaja	*El siglo XVIII*
L. M. de Lojendio	*Gonzalo de Córdoba*
R. Menéndez Pidal	*Historia de España*
S. de Madariaga	*España*

Acknowledgements

The authors wish to acknowledge permission to reproduce the following copyright material:

Margery Allingham, *More Work for the Undertaker* by permission of Curtis Brown Ltd.

Kingsley Amis, *Lucky Jim* by permission of Victor Gollancz Ltd.

Enid Bagnold, *National Velvet* by permission of William Heinemann Ltd.

James Baldwin, *Another Country* by permission of John Farquharson Ltd.

D. Barrington Haynes, *Glass Through the Ages* by permission of Penguin Books Ltd.

H. E. Bates, *Fair Stood the Wind for France* (Michael Joseph Ltd.) and *The Poacher* (Jonathan Cape Ltd.) by permission of Laurence Pollinger Ltd.

Jeremy Bernstein, *The Analytical Engine* by permission of Martin Secker & Warburg Ltd.

Maud Bodkin, *Archetypal Patterns in Poetry* by permission of Oxford University Press.

Gertrude and Muirhead Bone, *Days in Old Spain* by permission of Macmillan & Co. Ltd.

Dietrich Bonhoeffer, *No Rusty Swords* by permission of Collins Publishers.

John Bowen, *The Birdcage* by permission of Faber & Faber Ltd.

Francis Brett Young, *The Tragic Bride* by permission of C. Combridge Ltd.

Brigid Brophy, *Flesh* by permission of Martin Secker & Warburg Ltd.

Tyrrell Burgess, *A Guide to English Schools* by permission of Penguin Books Ltd.

C. A. Burland, *Man and Art* by permission of Studio Vista Ltd.

Truman Capote, *In Cold Blood* Copyright © 1966 by Truman Capote. By permission of Hamish Hamilton, London.

Joyce Cary, *To be a Pilgrim* by permission of Curtis Brown Ltd.

Henry Cecil, *Sober as a Judge* by permission of Michael Joseph Ltd.

Camilo José Cela, *La familia de Pascual Duarte* by permission of Ediciones Destino.

Raymond Chandler, 'The Big Sleep' from *The Raymond Chandler Omnibus* Copyright © 1953 by Raymond Chandler (Hamish Hamilton, London).

Kenneth Clark, *Landscape into Art* by permission of John Murray (Publishers) Ltd.

James A. Coleman, *Relativity for the Layman* by permission of the author.

R. G. Collingwood, *The Principles of Art* by permission of Clarendon Press.

Cyril Connolly, *The Rock Pool* by permission of Hamish Hamilton Ltd.

Joseph Conrad, '*Twixt Land and Sea* by permission of J. M. Dent & Sons Ltd. and the Trustees for the Joseph Conrad Estate.

Edmund Crispin, *Holy Disorders* by permission of Edmund Crispin and Victor Gollancz Ltd.

P. M. de Artinaño, *Metalwork* by permission of Burlington Magazine Publications Ltd.

Miguel Delibes, *La sombra del ciprés es alargada* by permission of Ediciones Destino.

Henry de Montherlant, *The Bachelors* by permission of Weidenfeld & Nicolson Ltd.

Daphne du Maurier, *Jamaica Inn* by permission of Curtis Brown Ltd.

Gerald Durrell, *The Bafut Beagles* by permission of Rupert Hart-Davis Ltd.

Lawrence Durrell, *Balthazar*, *Clea* and *Bitter Lemons* each by permission of Faber & Faber Ltd.

William Empsom, *Seven Types of Ambiguity* by permission of Chatto & Windus Ltd.

Benjamin Farrington, *Greek Science* by permission of Penguin Books Ltd.

Ortega y Gasset, *La rebelión de las masas* by permission of Revista de Occidente.

F. H. George, *Automation, Cybernetics and Society* by permission of International Textbook Co. Ltd.

William Golding, *Lord of the Flies* by permission of Faber & Faber Ltd.

L. Goldsheider, *El Greco* by permission of Phaidon Press Ltd.

Elizabeth Goudge, *Green Dolphin Country* by permission of Hodder & Stoughton Ltd. and *Towers in the Mist* by permission of Gerald Duckworth & Co. Ltd.

Nigel Grant, *Soviet Education* by permission of Penguin Books Ltd.

Sir Alister Hardy, *The Living Stream* and *The Divine Flame* by permission of Collins Publishers.

Richard Hoggart, *The Uses of Literacy* by permission of Chatto & Windus Ltd.

E. J. Holmyard, *Alchemy* by permission of Penguin Books Ltd.

A. Hopkins, *Talking About Symphonies* by permission of Heinemann Educational Books Ltd.

Joris-Karl Huysmans, *The Paintings of Grünewald* by permission of Phaidon Press Ltd.

Aldous Huxley, *Brave New World* by permission of Mrs. Laura Huxley and Chatto & Windus Ltd.

I.C.I. Fibres Division, *Making-up Processes* by permission of I.C.I. Fibres Ltd.

Arthur Jacobs, *Choral Music* by permission of Penguin Books Ltd.

Howard Jones, *Crime in a Changing Society* by permission of Penguin Books Ltd.

Spencer Jones, *Worlds Without End* by permission of Hodder & Stoughton Ltd.

Stephen Joseph, *The Playhouse in England* by permission of Barrie & Jenkins Ltd.

James Joyce, *The Dubliners* by permission of Jonathan Cape Ltd.

C. G. Jung, *Psychology and Religion: West and East* (Routledge & Kegan Paul, 1958) Vol. II of *The Collected Works of C. G. Jung* (Copyright the Bollingen Foundation).

Nikos Kanzantzakis, *Zorba the Greek* by permission of Bruno Cassirer Ltd.

E. Lafuente, *Velazquez* by permission of Phaidon Press Ltd.

Stanley Lane-Poole, *The Moors in Spain* by permission of Ernest Benn Ltd.

E. V. Lucas, Committees from *Visibility Good* by permission of Methuen & Co. Ltd.

Arnold Lunn and Garth Lean, *The New Morality* by permission of Blandford Press Ltd.

Colin MacInnes, *June in Her Spring* by permission of MacGibbon & Kee.

Ana María Matute, *Fiesta al noroeste* by permission of Ediciones Destino.

Alice Meynell, 'Waterfalls' in *Modern English Essays* 2nd series (O.U.P.) by permission of Mrs. Sylvia Mulvey acting for Alice Meynell's executors.

Nicholas Monsarrat, *The Cruel Sea* (Cassell & Co. Ltd.) by permission of Mr. Nicholas Monsarrat.

Alberto Moravia, *Bitter Honeymoon* by permission of Martin Secker & Warburg Ltd.

Iris Murdoch, *A Severed Head* by permission of the author, and Chatto & Windus Ltd.

V. S. Naipaul, *An Area of Darkness* by permission of Andre Deutsch Ltd.

Bernard Newman, *Both Sides of the Pyrenees* by permission of Barrie & Jenkins Ltd.

Thomas W. Ogletree, *The 'Death of God' Controversy* by permission of S. C. M. Press Ltd.

Geoffrey Parrinder, *The World's Living Religions* by permission of Pan Books Ltd.

Alan Paton, *Debbie Go Home* by permission of Jonathan Cape Ltd.

Ronald Peacock, *The Art of Drama* by permission of Routledge & Kegan Paul Ltd.

Ramón Menéndez Pidal, *The Cid and his Spain* by permission of John Murray (Publishers) Ltd.

Frederick Raphael, *Earlsdon Way* by permission of Cassell & Co. Ltd.

Herbert Read, *Concise History of Modern Painting* by permission of Thames & Hudson Ltd.

W. J. Reichmann, *Use and Abuse of Statistics* by permission of Methuen & Co. Ltd.

Douglas Rhymes, *No New Morality* by permission of Constable & Co. Ltd.

Bertrand Russell, *Mysticism and Logic* by permission of George Allen & Unwin Ltd.

John Russell Taylor, 'John Huston' by permission of *The Times*.

Göran Schildt, *The Wake of Odysseus* translated by Alan Blair by permission of the author and translator.

Captain Robert F. Scott, *The Voyage of the 'Discovery'* by permission of John Murray (Publishers) Ltd.

Scott Fitzgerald, *The Great Gatsby* in *The Bodley Head Scott Fitzgerald, Volume I* by permission of The Bodley Head.

C. P. Snow, *The Masters* and *Corridors of Power* by permission of The Macmillan Company of Canada Ltd. and Macmillan & Co. Ltd.

Muriel Spark, *The Mandlebaum Gate* by permission of Harold Ober Associates Incorporated. Copyright © 1965 by Muriel Spark.

Walter Starkie, *Road to Santiago* by permission of John Murray (Publishers) Ltd.

John Steinbeck, *The Winter of our Discontent* and *Tortilla Flat* by permission of William Heinemann Ltd.

Denys Sutton, 'Goya as a Portraitist' by permission of Apollo Magazine Ltd.

Ladislav Tauc, 'Actividad funcional de la neurona de los moluscas' by permission of *Endeavour*.

Dylan Thomas, *Portrait of the Artist as a Young Dog* by permission of J. M. Dent & Sons Ltd. and the Trustees for the Copyrights of the late Dylan Thomas.

Flora Thompson, *Lark Rise to Candleford* by permission of Oxford University Press.

James Thurber, *Vintage Thurber* Copyright © 1963 Hamish Hamilton Ltd.

Teilhard de Chardin, *Hymn of the Universe* and *The Phenomenon of Man* by permission of Collins Publishers.

Stephen Toulmin and June Goodfield, *The Architecture of Matter* by permission of Hutchinson & Co. Ltd.

G. M. Trevelyan, *English Social History* by permission of Longman Group Ltd.

Helen Waddell, *Peter Abelard* by permission of Constable & Co. Ltd.

Hugh Walpole, *Judith Paris* and *Rogue Herries* by permission of Sir Rupert Hart-Davis.

J. Wells, *A Short History of Rome* by permission of Methuen & Co. Ltd.

Morris West, *Children of the Sun* by permission of William Heinemann Ltd.

Rebecca West, *The Birds Fall Down* by permission of A. D. Peters & Co. Ltd.

William H. Whyte, *The Organization Man* (Jonathan Cape Ltd.) by permission of Laurence Pollinger Ltd.

Charles Williams, *All Hallows Eve* (Faber & Faber Ltd.) by permission of David Higham Associates, Ltd.

Bernard Wolfe, *Limbo '90* by permission of Martin Secker & Warburg Ltd.

Virginia Woolf, *The Waves* by permission of Quentin Bell, Angelica Garnett, and the Hogarth Press.

John Wyndham, *The Midwich Cuckoos* (Michael Joseph Ltd.) by permission of David Higham Associates Ltd.

John Wyndham and Lucas Parkes, *The Outward Urge* (Michael Joseph Ltd.) by permission of David Higham Associates Ltd.